NOAH
AND THE GREAT FLOOD

NOAH AND THE GREAT FLOOD

The Proof And Effects Of It

By
Jerry Blount

Published by Gatekeeper Press
3971 Hoover Rd. Suite 77
Columbus, OH 43123-2839
www.GatekeeperPress.com

Copyright © 2017 by Jerry Blount

All rights reserved. Neither this book, nor any parts within it may be sold or reproduced in any form without permission.

ISBN: 9781619846678
eISBN: 9781619846661

Printed in the United States of America

CONTENTS

INTRODUCTION 7

CHAPTER 1 Can we Believe the Bible About the flood 11

CHAPTER 2 The Reason for the Flood 15

CHAPTER 3 The Population of the World Before the Flood 19
    Pre-flood Cities 22

CHAPTER 4 Knowledge Before the Flood 25
    The Sumerian King List 28
    Pre-flood Seals 29
    The Code of Hammurabi 30

CHAPTER 5 The Earth Before the Flood 31

CHAPTER 6 The Climate Before the Flood 35

CHAPTER 7 The Construction of the Ark 41

CHAPTER 8 The Animals in the Ark 45

CHAPTER 9 The Duration of the Flood 49

CHAPTER 10 The Depth of the Flood 53

CHAPTER 11 The Biblical Account of the Flood 55
    The Atrahasis Epic---The Babylonian Genesis 58
    Enuma Elish--The Mesopotamian Creation 59
    The Chaldean Account 59
    The Gilgamesh Account 60

CHAPTER 12 The Biblical Evidence of the Flood 63

CHAPTER 13 The Case for a Worldwide Flood 67

CHAPTER 14 The Changes to the Earth's Strata 71

CHAPTER 15 The Changes to the Earth 81

CHAPTER 16 The Bible VS Evolution Uniformitarianism 89

CHAPTER 17 The Fossil Record 111
    Living Fossils 119

CHAPTER 18 Dating Methods 127
    The Geological Column 131

CHAPTER 19 How Old is the Earth 139
    Did God Create a Mature Earth 149

CHAPTER 20 Dinosaurs and Man 153

CHAPTER 21 The Ice Age 167

CHAPTER 22 Noah's Sacrifice and God's Covenant 173

CHAPTER 23 Where is the Ark, Has it Been Found 175

CHAPTER 24 God's Final Judgment 189

PHOTOS & ILLUSTRATIONS 193

BIBLIOGRAPHY 195

INTRODUCTION

THE STORY OF NOAH, the ark, and the great flood is probably as well-known as any story in history. It has captured our imagination as adults as well as children. Nearly every culture has their version of a global flood. Global flood stories have been documented in almost every region of the world. Ancient civilizations such as in (Europe, Africa, the Near East, China and Asia, North, Central and South America, Australia, the Pacific Islands) all have their stories of the great flood. The flood is by far the most significant event in history between the time of creation and the coming of Christ. A third of human history, 2000 years, is recorded in the first eleven chapters of Genesis. The events of the flood fill more than a third of those eleven chapters. More chapters are devoted to Noah and the flood than was dedicated to the creation record. It's that important to God that we know the facts. Other than creation, the flood was the greatest event in the history of our earth. It marked the end of the world of transcendent beauty and perfection that God had created for the abode of man. The topography and condition of the earth after the flood was a much harsher environment for the existence of man. The glory of God's perfect creation no longer existed.

There are repeated references of the flood throughout the Old and New Testaments. In the New Testament, Jesus and the disciples hold it up as a warning of God's wrath against sin. The flood was a preview for the final coming judgment (2 Peter 3:6-7). We need to know that it was a real event and the reason for it.

Old world missionaries reported their amazement at finding remote tribes already possessing legends with tremendous similarities to the Bible's accounts of the worldwide flood. *H.S. Bellamy in Moons, Myths and Men* estimates that altogether there are over 500 Flood legends worldwide.

"These flood tales are frequently linked by common elements that parallel the Biblical account including the warning of the coming flood, the construction of a boat in advance, the storage of animals, the inclusion of family, and the release of birds to determine if the water level had subsided. The overwhelming consistency among flood legends found in distant parts of the globe indicates they were derived from the same origin, but oral transcription has changed the details through time." [1]

I realize that at the current time, it would be impossible to write about the Flood, without it creating controversy. Especially, if one is writing that the Biblical account of the flood is true, when there are so many from the scientific community claiming there was no global flood. I only ask that you read this book with an open mind and not put any limits on the all-powerful God, simply because it might not fit into our conventional thinking. Our God would not have devoted so much of the Bible to the flood if he didn't want us to know the real facts.

If you consider that nearly every part of the world has their version of the global flood and that most of the earth's surface, even on the mountaintops is made up of sedimentary bedrock. Obviously, there was a global flood. Like the old saying goes; *"if it looks like a duck, walks like a duck and quacks like a duck, then it is undoubtedly a duck."*

For centuries man never questioned the Biblical teaching that the flood was a global flood and that the earth was six thousand or so years old. It was an accepted fact that the sedimentary rock that covered the surface, along with the fossils entombed within it was the results of the catastrophic conditions of a worldwide flood. For many this view has changed over the last two centuries with the development of the theory of uniformitarianism by men like Lydell and Hutton. They held that the natural forces now changing the shape of the earth's surface were operating in the past in the same manner. In other words, the present is the key to understanding the past. They believe that by studying the natural processes of today, they can interpret the past. They assume that the natural processes have never changed from the beginning of time.

---

1   N.W. Creation Network, *Flood Legends from Around the World*

This revolutionary idea was instrumental in leading Charles Darwin to his theory of biological evolution in the 1830's.

The fact that these opinions were developed in the name of science and had been presented as scientific facts have advanced them to the point that they are being taught in the schools as if they are indeed fact. In actuality, the theory of evolutionary uniformitarianism cannot be proven, any more than the Biblical flood account of a catastrophic event can be shown by man's limited knowledge.

The very thought of a universal flood is abhorrent to the evolutionist. A worldwide flood undermines their theory that the earth's strata were laid down over an extremely lengthy process of sedimentation and erosion. A process that they claim took millions and even billions of years. They believe that anything is possible if given enough time, even evolution. Therefore it is imperative that earth has a history of millions of years, for their theory to have any credibility.

They adamantly deny that a universal flood ever happened. Even though a global flood of the magnitude that the Bible speaks of could have accomplished the same changes to the earth's surface in a rather short period, rather than the billions of years they claim it took.

They deny that there was ever a worldwide flood even though nearly 90% of the earth's surface is made up of sedimentary bedrock, indicating that the earth was indeed covered with water at some time.

The Apostle Peter must have foreseen this day coming for he writes;

> *"Knowing this first: that scoffers will come in the last days, walking according to their own lusts, and saying, "Where is the promise of His coming? For since the fathers fell asleep, all things continue as they were from the beginning of creation." For this they willfully forget: that by the word of God the heavens were of old, and the earth standing out of the water and in the water, by which the world that then existed perished, being flooded with water. But the heavens and the earth which are now preserved by the same word, are reserved for fire until the day of judgment and perdition of ungodly men." (2 Peter 3:3-7) (NKJV)*

Did Peter foresee the theory of uniformitarianism? The theory that the natural processes taking place have remained the same from the beginning of time, and that observing the present is the key to the past. Undoubtedly he did, for as you read verse four, he writes that scoffers will say: "*all things continue as they were from the beginning of creation.*" Verse five tells us that they will deny that God created all things. They deny the fact that God judged and cleansed the earth by water (vs. 6). They deny that He will again judge and cleanse the earth again by fire (vs. 7). Peter speaks of the heavens (atmosphere and celestial) and earth of old before the flood. Peter is warning us that a new philosophy will develop in the last days. A philosophy that will deny that God created the world. They will deny God's judgment upon the earth by the flood. And by denying the judgment by water, they will no longer believe in the coming judgment by fire. Indeed, this is precisely the philosophy we see taking place in the world today.

The earth before the flood was a vastly different, climatically and geologically world than we live in today. Our earth was changed drastically by the flood, as we shall see. The judgment by water was just as complete as the judgment by fire will be, with the exception that after the judgment by fire, Satan will be dealt with permanently.

CHAPTER 1

Can We Believe the Bible about the Flood

I AM WRITING THIS FROM the standpoint that the Bible is 100% true. That the scriptures, while written by man were God inspired. I have been completely through the Bible scores of times. I have spent over fifty years reading, studying, researching and teaching the scriptures. I believe the Bible to be the absolute word of God. But, that of course is only my opinion. There is, however, an enormous amount of evidence that proves the scriptures to be reliable and accurate.

Over 25% of the Bible is made up of prophecy. Over 2000 of these prophecies have been fulfilled, many down to very specific details. None of the books from the other religions have dared to make such predictions as the Bible contains, for who but God, knows the future.

There are 330 prophecies concerning the Messiah that were fulfilled by the coming and life of Jesus. No theologian or historian of credibility denies that Jesus lived and fulfilled the prophecies.

Mathematician Professor Peter Stoner and his class done the calculations concerning eight major prophecies about Jesus. They found that the chance that any man might have lived to the present time and fulfilled all eight prophecies is 1 in 100,000,000,000,000,000. Or to put it in perspective, Stoner determined that it would be like covering the state of Texas two feet deep in quarters, mark one quarter, bury it somewhere in Texas, blindfold a person and tell him to find it on the first try.[2]

---

2   Stoner, Peter W., *Science Speaks*, Chicago, Moody Press, 1969

They determined that the odds for someone to fulfill 48 of the prophecies were 1 in 13 trillion. Amazing isn't it that Jesus not only fulfilled those 48 prophecies but he fulfilled over three hundred Biblical prophecies concerning his life. God did not intend that there be any mistake about who the Messiah was.

It is inconceivable that any skeptic could honestly deny the overwhelming evidence for the reliability and accuracy of the Bible. The Bible is much more than just another human document; it is the infallible, God-given record of the earth, man and his relationship with his creator.

Archaeology has continued to prove the accuracy of the scriptures. Over 25,000 archeological discoveries, have verified the accuracy of the Bible. The Dead Sea scrolls among other discoveries have shown that the scriptures have remained virtually unchanged from the beginning. Archaeologists continue to find evidence that document the accuracy of the scriptures.

Critics claimed that the Biblical King David never existed. Recent discoveries have confirmed, however, that he did exist. In 1993 archaeologist site surveyor Gila Cook accidentally discovered an inscribed stone within a newly excavated wall in Israel. The writing on the stone contains the historical evidence of King David. In 2014 six seals were discovered which offer additional proof to the kingdoms of David and Solomon.

New discoveries are continuing to prove the accuracy of the Bible. In fact, all archaeology finds have agreed with the biblical, historical accounts as recorded in the Bible. There has not been a single artifact or discovery made that would disprove what is written in The Word of God.

The Bible contains information that could not have been written without divine inspiration. The Bible's main theme is the salvation of man. However, the scriptures also include wisdom and advanced knowledge about nature, prophecy, medical, sanitation and science. Knowledge that was thousands of years ahead of its time proving that the Scriptures were God inspired.

The fact that Jesus lived is a part of history that nobody denies. His teaching is a part of recorded history. Many times Jesus quoted scripture or spoke of events in the Old Testament. When Jesus talked of Noah and the flood, it was apparent that he knew it was an actual event that had taken place.

"As it was in the days of Noah, so it will be at the coming of the Son of Man. For in the days before the flood, people were eating and drinking, marrying and giving in marriage, up to the day Noah entered the ark; and they knew nothing about what would happen until the flood came and took them all away." (Matthew 24:37-39)

If Jesus knew the scripture concerning the flood were accurate, should we not believe it also? If there is proof that much of the Bible is true, why would we doubt parts of it? Jesus's teaching of the scriptures was infallible. Since Jesus spoke of the flood as a real event, we can believe without reservation that it did indeed take place.

We will touch more on the proof that the Bible is the divine word of God in the chapter "The Biblical Evidence of the Flood."

CHAPTER 2

The Reason for the Flood

THE FOLLOWING SCRIPTURES AND the identity of the Nephilim and sons of God has been discussed and debated for years.

> "1. When human beings began to increase in number on the earth and daughters were born to them. 2. the sons of God saw that the daughters of humans were beautiful, and they married any of them they chose. 3. Then the Lord said, "My Spirit will not contend with humans forever, for they are mortal; their days will be a hundred and twenty years,"
>
> 4. The Nephilim were on the earth in those days--and also afterward--when the sons of God went to the daughters of humans and had children by them. They were heroes of old, men of renown.
>
> 5. The Lord saw how great the wickedness of the human race had become on the earth, and that every inclination of the thoughts of the human heart was only evil all the time." *(Genesis 6:1-6)*

There are different views concerning the identity of the Nephilim and sons of God. One view is that the sons of God refers to fallen angels. There is several problems with this view, one being that God himself had used, 'sons of God' when referring to Godly men. Some scriptures referring to man as sons of God are:

"Blessed are the peacemakers, for they will be called the sons of God" (Matthew 5:9).

"You are all sons of God through faith in Jesus Christ" (Galatians 3:26).

"those who are led by the spirit of God are sons of God" (Romans 8:14).

Jesus stated in Mark 12:25 that angels do not marry. This verse alone would seem to disprove this view. Another point is that the scriptures declare that God was greatly grieved by man. It was man that God regretted creating, and man that God destroyed. There was no reference or mention of angels.

Another view is that the Nephilim were giants, possibly half human and half angel. The term Nephilim is unclear in the definition. It is related to the verb "to fall" (naphal) in Hebrew, which could just refer to fallen man. The King James Version translates it as giants from the influence of the Latin Vulgate term gigantes. The context of Genesis 6 does not reveal they were giants. There may have been some influence on the Latin Vulgate by the Septuagint's (Greek translation of the Old Testament about 200–300 years before Christ) use of Greek word gigentes. This view is strictly conjecture and lacks any credibility. Some commentators maintain that the original meaning of Nephilim or Giants was that they were tyrants, brigands, and thugs, (those that prey upon others).

The view shared by most Bible scholars today is that the sons of God were the Sethites (descendants of Adam's son Seth). These were godly men from the line of Adam to Seth and down to Noah, who followed the ways of God.

The Nephilim were those who had fallen away; they were the Canaanites (descendants of Cain). The Canaanites turned away from God in the very beginning. Polygamy began with Cain himself. Lamech, from the line of Cain, killed a young man and boasted of it to his wives in song. The Canaanites were a wicked and evil people, with no desire to do good and follow the ways of God. They yielded to the lust of the eye and the flesh, to violence and greed. They lived without moral restraints of any kind.

Eventually, the godly men, (Sethites), had relations with ungodly women of the Canaanites and were lead away from the path of righteousness. Their offspring followed after the Canaanites and fell away from the Godly life their ancestors had lived. The line of Seth, the children of God, became like the children of men, wicked and worldly until it was only Noah and his family that still walked with the Lord.

The people before the flood were a progressive people with significant cultural and material achievements, however, at heart, they were a godless and materialistic people.

Leonard Woolley, in describing the graves which he uncovered below the flood sediment stated *"In no single grave has there been any figure of a god, any symbol or ornament that strikes one as being of a religious nature"*.[3] Idolatry apparently did not take place before the flood. It is not mentioned in the scriptures until after the flood.

One fact is very clear; mankind had fallen so low that there was no good left in him. Verse 6, says that he was evil all the time. The wickedness of man had become so bad that the Lord was sorry he had created man. Only Noah found favor in the eyes of the Lord. If it was not for Noah, God very likely would have completely wiped man from the face of the earth.

> *"The Lord saw how great the wickedness of the human race had become on the earth, and that every inclination of the thoughts of the human heart was only evil all the time. The Lord regretted that he had made human beings on the earth, and his heart was deeply troubled. So the Lord said, "I will wipe from the face of the earth the human race I have created--and with them the animals, the birds and the creatures that move along the ground--for I regret that I have made them," But Noah found favor in the eyes of the Lord," (Genesis 6:5-8)*

Can you imagine a world where man's thoughts are evil all the time? Where there is no good to be found in him. Man had sunk into total depravity. Violence, sexual perversion, hatred and wickedness had become commonplace. In Genesis 6:11, God said that the world was full of violence, he then repeats it again in verse 13. The fact that God repeated it two verses later tells us that the world was a very violent place. With the violence, we would associate killings, robberies, rape, aggressive behavior and all the other things we

---

3 Woolley, Leonard, *Ur of The Chaldees*, InExile Publishing, 2012

connect to violent conduct. Only Noah and his family still followed God. Noah was a preacher (2 Peter 2:5) of the righteousness of God. He was 480 years old before he started to build the Ark. During that time, only his family listened to him and followed God. For 120 years as Noah built the Ark, he tried to convince the people to turn to God and forsake their evil ways, all to no avail. Noah warned them that if they didn't turn to God, they would be destroyed by the flood waters. In return, he only received their laughter. How do you convince the people there is going to be a flood, in a land where it had never rained? It is hard to imagine the persistence and patience that was required of Noah to continue. Of the millions of people on earth at the time only seven listened to him and followed God. As I stated before, if not for Noah, God may have completely wiped mankind from the face of the earth forever.

CHAPTER 3

The Population of the World before the Flood

THE BOOK OF GENESIS begins with the creation story. Only three chapters later we read about the fall of man. And by chapter six we are learning about the events concerning Noah and the flood. only two chapters separate the fall of man and the story of the flood. These two chapters deal mainly with genealogically. Because of the two events, along with the creation story, are so close together in the Bible. We tend to think of that period as having been much shorter than it was. Surprisingly, a third of human history is documented in just the first eleven chapters of Genesis.

We have an exact chronology, in chapter five of Genesis. According to this chronology the Flood occurred 1656 years after creation. This is confirmed by the genealogical table in chapter one of First Chronicles, and again in Luke 3:23-38.

To put 1656 years in perspective, if we were to go back 1656 years from our present time, we would only be in the third century A.D.

The general view is that the population before the flood was quite small and limited mostly to the Mesopotamian area. This was not the case. Conservatively speaking, the population would have been in the millions.

Even in our present age, 1656 years is sufficient time for the human race to grow to an enormous population. The antediluvian man lived to an average age of nine hundred years. It stands to reason that he was much greater in vitality than we are today. Therefore, we can assume that he was much more prolific also. Add to this the abundant food supply, and you have ideal conditions for very rapid growth in population.

With the mild climate and abundant plant and animal life worldwide, it would be foolish to think that a population numbering in the millions would not have spread out over the greater portion of the earth as God had commanded. It would stand to reason that since the flood covered the whole earth, man must have inhabited most of it. It would seem unlikely that God's judgment would have been upon the entire earth if mankind and his wickedness was confined to one small area.

God's first words to Adam and Eve after blessing them were "*Be fruitful and increase in number; fill the earth and subdue it.*" (Genesis 1:28) A rapidly expanding population seemed to be the order especially considering mankind lived for hundreds of years.

Adam lived nine hundred and thirty years and lived to see his children's children to the eighth generation. Adam lived as a contemporary of Lamech, Noah's father for fifty-six years. Noah lived for nine hundred and fifty years and spent the last fifty-eight years of his life as a contemporary of Abraham. Noah saw his children's children to the tenth generation.

In his book '*All About The Bible*', Sidney Collett calculated the population of the antediluvian civilization. Based on the pre-flood average age, (excluding Enoch, who was taken up to heaven without dying at the age of three hundred and sixty-five), was nine hundred years. For comparison, he used the average age and the number of children at the time of his study. Comparing the average age of seventy, with the nine hundred years average age would equal out to one hundred and twenty children per family. Being conservative, and to arrive at an estimate so moderate that, startling as it was, it would nevertheless commend itself to the general acceptance of his readers. Collett used the figure of forty-eight for the number of children per family.

He allowed for the possibility that one-fourth of the population did not marry, although everyone whose name is given did marry. He also allowed for the premature death of another quarter of the population. The only early death we read about was Abel, although, in such a violent society, there were sure to be more.

He then assumed that only one-half of the actual population married and those, during the seven hundred out of the nine hundred years of their lives, had no children at all. They only had children during the second and third hundred years of their lives, and then at the average rate of only one child every four years.

Based on these moderate figures, he determined that during Adam's lifetime, the population of the world might well have reached nearly twenty million. And before Cain and Seth passed away, it might have been over one hundred and thirty-six million.[4]

Collett acknowledges that these figures were just speculation on his part, and did not represent an exact population of those times. The population could have been less, or it could have been much greater even than Collett's calculations. I believe that the population was probably considerable larger than Collett's estimate, considering how long people lived and the fact that it was 1656 years from the time of Adam to the flood. The Israelites were in Egypt for 430 years, (Exodus 12:40), and their numbers increased from seventy to two million, with normal lifespans.

If you simply figure that the average family numbered twenty children and using the ten generations of Genesis chapter five, you would have a population of two billion people. Considering that man lived for hundreds of years, I would think that a family of twenty would be a very conservative estimate. My grandparents on my mother's side had eighteen children. There can be no doubt, but that there would have been a very substantial population.

The prevalence of strife and violence would have encouraged the broad distribution of the people. It definitely would not have been a small populace contained within the Mesopotamia region, as some historians advocate. God said the world was a very violent place (Genesis 6:11, 13). Violence and fighting would have encouraged the dispersion of people throughout the earth. If there was a population of one or two billion, it could've easily have expanded worldwide. Our present global population did not reach one billion until the year 1804, and it grew to two billion in 1927.[5]

The population had unquestionably spread over the entire globe long before arriving at either of these milestones. God not only gave the command to increase and multiply but to fill the earth as well *"Be fruitful and increase in number; fill the earth and subdue it."* (Genesis 1:28)

---

4   Collett, Sidney, *All About The Bible*, Westwood, N.J., Barbour And Company, 1989.
5   Wikipedia, *World Population*, http://en.wikipedia.org/wiki/World_population, 2015

Dr, Henry Morris writes: "We are confident, therefore that our estimate of a population of one billion people on the earth at the time of the Deluge is very conservative; it could well have been far more than this. A population of this order of magnitude would certainly have spread far beyond the Mesopotamian plains, in fact, for all practical purposes, would have "filled the earth," as the scripture says."[6]

Preflood cities: The antediluvian population would have been more than large enough to have established many sizeable cities. However, as a result of the flood most signs of civilization were either destroyed or buried in hundreds or even thousands of feet of sediment. There had been very little found of the antediluvian (pre-flood) civilization. However, the city of Ur and other towns in Mesopotamia area that were in existence before the flood were an exception. They were apparently buried mostly intact in much less sediment than most areas. A tablet excavated at Nippur records several cities that existed before the Flood.

"In the ancient city of Nippur, a tablet was unearthed, which recounts the Sumerian version of the Great Deluge. This tablet contains a total of six columns of writing composed around the time of Hammurabi relying upon material, which is considerably older. In the first two columns of the tablet, there is a brief account of the founding of five cities, which they claim to have also been prediluvian cities, including Shurippak, which, according to the Sumerians, was the city, in which Utnapishtim (Noah) dwelt.

This Shurippak is presently known as Shuruppak and is one of the oldest cities of the ancient people of southern Babylonia, some eighteen miles northwest of Uruk.

Here, in this tablet, there is an actual account of cities, which were in existence, when the world was one landmass, prior to the Great Flood".[7]

Mesopotamia is the Greek name for all the country between the Euphrates River on the west and the Tigris River on the east. From time immemorial, this country was divided into two political regions. Assyria occupied the North, with its capital of Nineveh,

---

6 Whitcomb, John C. and Morris, Henry M., *The Genesis Flood*, Phillipsburg, N.J., Presbyterian And Reformed Publishing Co., 1989
7 Austin, Allen, *Antediluvian civilizations*, www.genesis.allenauston.net/antediluvian.htm., 2006

and Babylonia occupied the south, with its capital of Babylon. The southern part of Babylonia which touched the Gulf was also known at different periods in its history as Sumer, Akkad, and Chaldea. All three names covered the same area of the country. The capital of the part of Babylonia was Ur, one of the oldest cities in the world. Ur was a seaport at the mouth of the Euphrates River. It was a pre-flood city, destroyed by the flood and rebuilt just before the time of Abraham. During the time of the Patriarch, it was the greatest city in all of Babylonia. It was the center of world commerce, a city of great wealth, the greatest libraries, and at the same time, it was the religious center of the then civilized world, with the largest and most beautiful temples of the time. It was from this city that God called Abraham to the land of Canaan.[8]

Kish was another city destroyed by the deluge. The tablets stated that it was the first city to be rebuilt after the flood.[9]

Other famous cities of Babylonia which were excavated by the archaeologists are Nippur, Lagash, Larsa, Eridu, Erech, Fara, Accad and of course the great city of Babylon.[10]

---

8   Kinnaman, J.O., *Diggers For Facts*, Haverhill, MA., *Destiny Publishers*, 1945.
9   Ibid
10 Ibid

CHAPTER 4

Knowledge before the Flood

ADAM AND EVE WERE probably brilliant people. The evolutionistic view that people of that era were ignorant and lived like cave dwellers could not be farther from the truth. God created Adam and Eve as perfect human beings in His image. He created them as adults with an adult knowledge and intellect by God. They possessed an extensive knowledge of a language for communicating with God. The Bible tells us that Adam named all the animals. (Genesis 2:20) To be able to name all the animals, birds and other creatures and then be able to remember the names and descriptions of each, would require a high degree of intelligence. I doubt if there is anyone today capable of doing this. What effect did the fall of man have upon the mind of man? Were our understanding and thoughts much clearer then? Did man have perfect memory with total recall? Of course, we can't know the answer until we get to Heaven ourselves.

While Adam and Eve were created with an adult God-given knowledge, ensuing generations were taught by parents and others. Their knowledge may not have been as complete as Adam's and Eve's.

Undoubtedly, because of the violent nature of man after the fall of mankind, there would have been much fighting and violence. There were probably many that were driven away from society. Many more may have wandered off to explore new lands. These small bands could easily have regressed to the point to where they would have lived in caves and lived very simple lives. There is no doubt but that there were large segments that degenerated to a level of savagery. But concluding that the entire race evolved from a race of cave dwellers and savages is not a realistic view.

There are numerous examples of civilizations regressing in the world. For example, over a thousand years before the time of Christ, there was a progressive farming culture that existed in the southwest portion of the United States. It included Arizona, New Mexico, plus parts of surrounding states, including Mexico. They utilized a huge irrigation system, with canals up to twenty miles long, that watered thousands of acres of farmland. Along with the irrigation, they made use of several techniques of water harvesting and conservation, such as terracing, which created a very successful agriculture practice. They grew a variety of crops, including a maize that they adapted to hot and dry climates. Other crops included beans, squash, tobacco, and cotton among many. This culture after having existed for over 3000 years, disappeared by the fifteenth century, with the culture and people of the area reverting to mostly hunter-gatherers.

With a God-given intelligence for man's beginning and the commandant to subdue the world and possess it, we can only wonder about the knowledge that was lost because of the flood. It was a time when all the inhabitants of the world were one race, and all spoke the same language. There is evidence that man was highly sophisticated and possessed an advanced knowledge of the art of building, with which he built elaborate cities.

That man had considerable intelligence from the start is evident in chapter four of Genesis. In verse seventeen we read that Cain built a city and named it after his son Enoch (not to be confused with the Enoch from the line of Seth, which was taken up to heaven before he died). Later in the same chapter, we read: "Adah gave birth to Jabal; he was the father of those who lives in tents and raises livestock. His brother's name was Jubal; he was the father of all who plays stringed instruments and pipes. Zillah also had a son, Tubal-Cain, who forged all kinds of tools out of bronze and iron." In these verses alone we see that there was farmers, herders, musicians and metal workers.

Very little was known about antediluvian cities or artifacts before 1919 when Dr. R. H. Hall of the British Museum began his excavations at Ur. In 1922 Dr. C. L. Woolley, field director for the British and the University of Pennsylvania Museums, took over the work at Ur and continued until 1934. Dr. Woolley sank an exploratory well over seventy feet deep. This well went through the remains of the city dump, which gave the archaeologists a cross-sectional view of the life of the people of the city. This provided

surprising evidence to an advanced antediluvian civilization, as recounted by archaeologist K.O Kinnaman:
"As the workmen slowly dug their way down, they finally came to a layer of clean clay. They said that there was no use digging further, for they had come to the end of things; but Dr. Woolley persuaded them to go on. This stratum of clay is eight feet thick. When a hole was made through the stratum, everyone was amazed beyond expression, for there before their eyes were artifacts never beheld, even in type, by modern man. Here were artifacts which even with our vaunted abilities, we cannot duplicate today.

The archaeologists agree that this stratum of clay eight feet thick was laid down by that great catastrophe known as The Flood. The artifacts beneath this stratum all belong to the pre-Flood era. Further excavations beneath this clay stratum revealed the fact that there was a city there. In other words Ur was a city before the Flood, and the remains of this pre-Flood city are there to testify to the fact. The same stratum and artifacts, and cities beneath it, have been found at three places: Ur, Fara, and Kish. The civilization beneath the stratum is so radically different that we have no difficulty in knowing absolutely that the continuity of history was suddenly and terrifically broken, and never again re-established".[11]

"Woolley's conjecture of previous inhabitants suggested that if he dug deep enough beneath Ur, he might encounter the flood deposit.......he sank deep shafts that led him to the royal cemeteries. When opened, the tombs displayed an interment of king and queen accompanied by human sacrifice on an extravagant scale. The entire retinue of the ancient court--its servants, soldiers of the guard, musicians, the ox that pulled the funeral cart, the driver and grooms--had been laid out as if they had fallen asleep under a spell at the foot of the wooden bier upon which the monarch lay, with the queen on her own platform wearing a floral headdress made of paper-thin leaves and flowers of gold, silver, and electrum. Every individual appeared ready to accompany the regent into the afterlife. To Woolley's experienced eye the grave objects expressed an art form and metallurgy so advance that they could not have been achieved without a long period of

---

11 Kinnaman, *J.O., Diggers For Facts*, Haverhill, MA., Destiny Publishers, 1945.

gestation. Even the architecture was revolutionary in its use of the arch, vault, and dome--inventions that would not reappear outside of Mesopotamia until the time of the Romans almost forty centuries later.......It was on his way through these strata that Woolley encountered the material evidence of a great inundation, represented in ten continuous feet of waterborne silt devoid of human artifacts. The silt blanketed houses and temples. Given the overall flatness of the surrounding countryside, Woolley saw the substantial thickness of this sterile deposit as evidence of a wide expanse of submergence".[12]

"The contents of the tombs illustrate a very highly developed state of society of an urban type, a society in which the architect was familiar with all the basic principles of construction known to us today. The artist, capable at time of a most vivid realism, followed for the most part standards and conventions whose excellence had been approved by many generations working before him; the craftsman in metal possessed a knowledge of metallurgy and a technical skill which few ancient people ever rivaled; the merchant carried on a far flung trade and recorded his transactions in writing; the army was well organized and victorious; agriculture prospered, and great wealth gave scope to luxury."[13]

"Man before the flood had not only multiplied and become a great people, but had also taken possession of the earth and had reached a high stage of civilization and culture. He had achieved great things. It was the golden age in the history of man, of which the various mythologies of later ages are but a faint and indistinct echo." [14]

Most modern day geologist, being uniformitarians, claim these flood discoveries were from local floods. The scientific community is quick to dismiss any artifacts that do not agree with their presupposed interpretation of the history of the world, especially if it involves a global flood.

---

12   Ryan, William & Pittman, Walter, *Noah's Flood*, New York, Simon & Schuster, 1999
13   Leonard Woolley, *Ur to The Chaldees*, InExile Publishing, 2012
14   Alfred M. Rehwinkel, *The Flood,The Flood: In the Light of the Bible, Geology, and Archaeology*, St. Louis, Mo., Concordia Publishing House, 1951

The Sumerian King List: A 4,000 year old tablet that was excavated at the site of the ancient city Nippu is an ancient list of rulers of Mesopotamia, their names, their seat of power and the length of their reigns. It contains an antediluvian portion which lists eight kings that reigned prior to the flood. The Sumerian King List begins with the very origin of kingship, which is seen as a divine institution: "the kingship had descended from heaven". The rulers in the earliest dynasties are represented as having really long life spans which is evident by their long reigns. It makes reference to a cataclysmic flood as well. It is obvious that the kings list is documenting the same time period and events as the Biblical account and is strong evidence for the historicity of the book of Genesis. There are remarkable similarities between the Sumerian King List and accounts in Genesis. For example, Genesis tells the story of 'the great flood' and Noah's efforts to save all the different kinds of animals on Earth from destruction. Likewise, in the Sumerian King List, there is discussion of a great deluge: "the flood swept over the earth." Interestingly, between Adam and Noah there are eight generations, just as there are eight kings between the beginning of kingship and the flood in the Sumerian King List.

After the flood, the King List records kings who ruled for much shorter periods of time. Thus, the Sumerian King List not only documents a great flood early in man's history, but it also reflects the same pattern of decreasing longevity as found in the Bible-men had extremely long life spans before the flood and much shorter lifespans following the flood.[15]

Pre-flood Seals: Seals appear to have been in common use before the flood. Seals always stood for the name of some person, identifying ownership. They were used as a signature on contracts, letters and receipts. Each person had his seal, and no two were alike. Seals were carved on small pieces of stone. Pre Flood seals were found by Dr. Schmidt, at Fara, under the Flood layer and by Dr. Woolley at Ur.

A clay seal known as the Adam and Eve Temptation seal was discovered in Sumer, the site of the most ancient known civilization. It depicts a man and woman who are both reaching for

---

15 Bryant G. Wood, *Great discoveries in Biblical Archaeology: The Sumerian King List, B Spade 16:4, Fall 2003, p. 120*

the fruit of a tree. A serpent is shown behind the woman. Now kept in the famed British Museum, this 5,000-year-old seal pictures an event that wasn't written about until circa 1440 B.C. Some say this is a coincidence, while others believe the item proves that the seal's artist somehow knew about the temptation story of Adam and Eve before there was a written record.

Another Sumerian seal shows a naked man and woman bowing in humiliation and followed by a serpent or Adam and Eve's expulsion from the Garden of Eden (Genesis 3:23). This seal dates to about 3500 B.C. and is kept in the museum at the University of Pennsylvania. Many people believe that these seals are sufficient proof that the story of Adam and Eve, as related in the Bible, actually happened. [16]

The Code of Hammurabi: The Code of Hammurabi, while not a preflood document, does date back to the time of Abraham and shows how advanced the laws were at that time. The rapid advancement of mankind after the flood testifies that much of the pre-flood knowledge was retained and used to build a new civilization.

"Discovered by a French explorer in 1902 in Susa, dates back to the time of Abraham. This is the oldest known code of laws in the world, and it shows that for the people for whom it was made were already far advanced in civilization. It guarded against bribery of judges and witnesses in court, against careless medical practices, and against ignorant or dishonest building contractors, as well as against oppression of widows or orphans. Property rights, deeds, wills, marriage settlements and legal contracts were carefully safeguarded. A similar advanced civilization is found in China and India dating back to about the same period when these early civilizations flourished.

There is but one explanation for this rapid progress among the nations following the flood, and that is that they continued where the generation of Noah left off. They transplanted the civilization of the old world to the new, just as the early European immigrant brought with him the culture and civilization of his homeland to America to give it a fresh start in this new and virgin land."[17]

---

16 J. O. Kinnaman, *Digger For Facts*, Haverhill, MA., Destiny Publishers, 1945.
17 Alfred M. Rehwinkel, *The Flood,The Flood: In the Light of the Bible, Geology, and Archaeology*, St. Louis, Mo., Concordia Publishing House, 1951

CHAPTER 5

The Earth before the Flood

TO UNDERSTAND THE SCOPE of the catastrophe effect of the flood upon the earth, we must first understand what the heavens and the earth were like before the flood.

On the sixth day God looked at all he had created and declared it good. If God said it was very good, then it was perfect. God had created the perfect environment for man to live in. Everything was perfect. It was truly a paradise, made just for mankind to enjoy.

"It was perfect in every detail. There were no thorns or thistles in the world. The earth brought forth abundantly of everything that was needful to provide for the wants, comforts, and pleasures of man. There was no need for a struggle for an existence either between man and man or between the beasts and their companions. There were no Saharas, no barren wastes, no disease breeding heat of the tropics. The most enchanting islands in the subtropical areas of the South Seas today are but an imperfect replica of what that world was which received the verdict "very good" from its creator."[18]

With the fall of Adam and Eve, sin entered the world. And with sin came the curse and the blight upon the earth. While the curse upon the world was immediate, not all of its consequences were immediately apparent. The planet still retained much of the glory of God's creation. The land was much more habitable than what exist now. The climate was a consistently mild climate that extended over the whole earth. Before the flood, there was no rainfall. Therefore there would have been no erosion of the topsoil. The soil was fertile,

---

18 Alfred M. Rehwinkel, *The Flood: In the Light of the Bible, Geology, and Archaeology,* St. Louis, Mo., Concordia Publishing House, 1951

perfect for growing, just as God had created it. The land mass was much greater in size and was connected. Roughly one-half of the earth's surfaces were land. There were no deserts, swamps or wastelands of any kind. What mountains that did exist were smaller and easier to navigate. In comparison, only a little more than one-fourth of the globe today is not covered with water and not all of that is suitable for man's habitation. The mountains of today are much larger, rocky barriers that separate regions and countries. They clearly affect the climate and biology of their respective areas. Remember the land that existed before the flood, was the same land that God had declared very good after creating it.

The antediluvian earth was just as God had created it. It was a very comfortable climate, where crops grew in perfect fertile soil and produced large harvests and livestock reproduced and grew fat on the abundant plant life. Maybe a glimpse of what the plant life was like, could be the single cluster of grapes that the Israelites brought back from Canaan which required two men to carry it, (Numbers 13;23-24). This took place after the flood, but it may provide an inkling of what plants were like before the deluge.

The fossil record testifies to the fact that plant life before the flood was much larger and more diverse than it is now.

"Not only was there a greater variety of plants, but the species still in existence were much larger and more widely distributed over the face of the earth; and there was an abundance and luxuriance of plant life in every part of the earth of which we today no longer are able to form an adequate conception." [19]

The world was a place rich in plant and animal life. It was a world which provided food in abundance for man or beast, with very little effort from either. It was a world that could support a population much greater than our present population. The billions of mammal fossils are ample evidence of the abundance of animals that inhabited the earth. Even though mankind had fallen, and man and the earth were now under the curse, it was still a veritable paradise compared to today's world. It was a world God had created for man's pleasure. It was a world God himself had declared was

---

19 Alfred M. Rehwinkel, *The Flood, The Flood: In the Light of the Bible, Geology, and Archaeology*, St. Louis, Mo., Concordia Publishing House, 1951

very good. But it was a world destined for destruction by the flood. It was a world to be destroyed by God, because of sin and man's rebellion. The Flood marked the end of the perfect world God had created for mankind.

If God had only wanted to destroy mankind and cleanse the earth of the sin and wickedness that had engulfed it, he could have done it without the violence nature of the flood. Why did God implement such drastic catastrophic changes to the earth, its climate, and its topography?

Due to the antediluvian earth's ideal climate and weather and the abundant harvests, life before the Flood would have been easy. Because life was comfortable and man had extra time for himself, he felt no inclination to be thankful to God. He turned from God and sought his own pleasures. He felt no need for God.

The earth that existed after the flood was much different from before. Now the land was rough, with huge mountain ranges, swamps, deserts, and all kinds of wastelands. There existed the Arctic and Antarctic poles and the steaming jungles of the Equator. There were now changing seasons with the winter's snow and cold, and the summer with its heat and humidity. Now there were violent storms with rain, lightning, and wind. Many wild animals were now dangerous to humans. Life on earth was no longer easy. Life was now a struggle to exist. Man no longer had lots of free time to seek his selfish pleasures.

When life is a struggle, or when we are going through struggles, we tend to be much more reliant on God. When life is comfortable, we sometimes forget we need God. I believe this is why God used the catastrophic flood to not only cleanse the world but also to alter the planet to reflect the state of man.

CHAPTER 6

The Climate before the Flood

THE PREFLOOD CLIMATE WAS a uniform mild and warm climate that existed over the entire globe. The temperatures extremes that we experience today did not exist. Neither did the seasonal changes that we are used to. Proof of this climate lies in the plant and animal fossil record, a record that does not lie.

"When nearly the same plants are found in Greenland and Guinea; when the same species, now extinct, are met with of equal development at the equator as at the poles, we cannot but admit that at this period the temperature of the globe was nearly alike everywhere.

What we now call climate was unknown in these geological times. There seems to only have been then only one climate over the whole globe."[20]

The fossil record shows that there was a mild uniform climate that existed over the whole world. Fossils have been found in great abundance in every part of the world. The flora and fauna fossils are an excellent thermometer with which to test the climate of any past period. The biological fossil evidence is unmistakable. Cold blooded reptiles cannot live in icy water or freezing conditions. And plants whose habitat is semi-tropical or temperate zone, cannot live and bear fruit or produce seeds and reproduce themselves under arctic conditions.

---

20 Samuel Kinns, *Moses and Geology: Or, the Harmony of the Bible with Science,* Ulan Press, 2012

Alfred R. Wallace, often referred to as the father of biogeography, stated: "There is but one climate known to the ancient fossil world as revealed by the plants and animals entombed in the rocks, and the climate was a mantle of springlike loveliness which seems to have prevailed continuously over the whole globe. Just how the world could have thus been warmed all over may be a matter of conjecture; that it was warmed effectively and continuously is a matter of fact."[21]

Another outstanding authority, Prof. George McCready Price writes:
"It would be quite useless to go through the whole fossiliferous series in order for there is not a single system which does not have coral limestone or other evidence of a mild climate way up north, most systems having such rock in the lands which skirt the very pole itself. The limestone and coal beds of the carboniferous period are the nearest known rocks to the North Pole. They crop out all around the polar basis; and from the dip of these beds, they must underlie the polar sea itself. But it is needless to go through the systems one after another, for they uniformly testify that a warm climate has in former times prevailed over the whole globe."[22]

"There would have been no white polar caps or reddish-brown desert regions, for thick green vegetation covered almost all of the land areas, even in polar regions (thick coal deposits have been discovered in the mountains of Antarctica."[23]

Fossils of plants and man-made implements found in the Sahara show that this great African desert was at one time covered with luxuriant vegetation and was inhabited by man. Similar remains have been discovered in the Gobi desert of China and the great desert areas of northwestern India. There were no deserts, swamps or other uninhabitable areas in the antediluvian world. It was still just as it was when God created it.

Not only was it a warm, mild climate, but it was a World without storms. No lightning, wind storms, thunderstorms, rain or snow. It did not rain, as the earth was watered by springs and rivers coming from out of the earth.

---

21 Alfred R. Wallace, *The Geographical Distribution of Animals,* London, Macmillan and Company, 1876
22 Prof. George McCready Price, *The New Geology,* Charleston, South Carolina, Nabu Press, 2014
23 John C. Whitcomb, *The Early Earth,* BMH Books, winona Lake, In., 2011 .

"but streams came up from the earth and watered the whole surface of the ground." (Genesis 2:6)

How was it possible for the whole world to have a mild warm climate when we have such diverse weather now? How could nature have functioned to produce conditions so different from those of today? How did things change?

Two possible theories that appears very plausible. The first is the canopy theory. The vapor canopy theory, not only answers the question of how it could be a mild climate worldwide, but it also answers other issues, such as how it could rain worldwide for such an extended period. It could also explain how people could live so long.

On the first day of creation, God divided the light from the darkness. These He divided into two relatively equal parts and call them day and night. On the second day, God divided the water into two parts. One part he put above the firmament and the other part was below it. Since God divided light and darkness into two equal parts, would it be too much to assume that he also divided the waters into two relatively equal parts? If this is true, then the amount of water that God placed above the firmament would have been much greater than what our present atmosphere contains. It would also mean that the oceans would have been much smaller than they are today. On the third day, God divided the land and water on the earth. The land and water would have been somewhat equal also. The same language was used in the division of light and darkness, the division of the waters, and the division of land and water. We know that light and darkness was divided equally. Therefore it is possible that all three were divided roughly equal. If this is true, it would certainly help explain some things.

A massive amount of water in the atmosphere would explain how it could rain hard for forty days and nights over the whole earth. Our present atmosphere doesn't begin to contain enough moisture for it to rain for such an extended period of time over the entire earth.

For this amount of water to stay aloft, it would have to be in the form of water vapor, possibly even extending out into space. As a vapor it would be transparent, allowing the sun, moon, and stars to shine through. It would have been much different than our thin atmosphere of today.

This vapor canopy would have had a profound effect on the earth's climate and living conditions. It would have ensured a mild, warm climate with only minor seasonal and latitudinal changes. This would seem to be logical, considering that God had originally intended man to live upon the earth naked. Adam and Eve were naked and apparently were not susceptible to heat, sunburn or the cold. They were naked until they ate from the tree of knowledge of good and evil and realized their sin. (Genesis 2:25)

The temperature of the earth would have been more consistent over the whole earth, instead of the extreme temperature difference between the equator and the north and south poles that we now experience with our present atmosphere.

For example, here's a very simple illustration, have you ever stood by a campfire on a chilly day? The part of you that faces the fire stays warm or even hot, while your other side that is away from the fire stays cold. It is the same with our current earth, the part that is nearest to the sun (the equator), stays warm while the part away from the sun (north and south poles), stay cold. Now think of that same campfire contained inside of a room. The temperature throughout the room would be fairly consistent, without the hot and cold differences. It would have been the same upon the earth at that time, because of the blanket of water vapor that shrouded the earth, would have acted as an insulating cover.

Another thought is that the heat that penetrated the canopy was diffused so equally over all the zones of latitude that the subtropical climate prevailed over the whole earth.

This water canopy could also have served as a protective measure against the sun's harmful ultraviolet radiations, which our present atmosphere only partially filters out. The present day adverse effects of the sun include sunburn, premature skin aging, skin damage, skin cancers, heat stress and heat stroke, cataracts, and immune suppression. The water vapor canopy would have filtered out these harmful effects.

Since it did not rain during this period (Genesis 2:5), there would not have been a need for the current wind patterns. Without wind or rain, there would not have been the storms spawning the lightning, hail, tornadoes, etc. that we experience today.

If you combine the lack of radiation and harmful effects of the present sun and the mild temperatures without the extreme heat and cold, it would have been a very pleasant time weatherwise to live. Could this be the reason for the longevity of life at that time? If you look at the lifespan of man after the flood, you will see that it began to decrease. There was a short time after the flood, when man lived for several hundred years, which is only natural that God would allow this to repopulate the earth. The fact that Egypt, Jordan, Canaan and the other areas where Abraham went were well populated and flourishing, testifies to the fact that there was a very rapid growth of the population after the flood. However, in only a few generations after the flood, man's lifespan had diminished to where it was nearly comparable to our present day life spans. Abraham was born only two hundred and ninety-two years after the flood, yet he was considered old and well stricken in age at one hundred. (Genesis 21:2,5)

Noah, at the age of nine hundred and fifty years, outlived the men of his generation. I imagine that God allowed this so that Noah might guide a new population in the ways of God.

The water canopy theory has been around for quite some time. Isaac Newton Vail published many pamphlets on the canopy theory, beginning with '*Waters Above The Firmament*' in 1874.[24]

The second theory is that the earth was tilted 23.5 degrees at the time of the flood. This tilting changed the earth's relation to the sun, which brought about our present climate zones. Before the deluge, the earth's axis was perpendicular to the plane of its orbit. Sunlight extended from pole to pole, creating a mild climate from pole to pole. Day and night were always equal in length at twelve hours each. All latitudes received the same amount of heat and light over the entire globe. The temperature remained constant year round, with the result that there was no change of seasons.

However, the axis of the Earth is not perpendicular to the plane of its orbit. The earth currently has an axial tilt, (also referred to as obliquity), of 23.5 degrees.

On December 21 the North Pole has turned away from the sun, and consequently the sun's rays fall short of it by 23.5 degrees. At the same time, they shine upon the South Pole. On June 21 the condition is reversed. The sun's rays now shine on the North Pole but fall short of the South Pole. Therefore the tilted axis of the earth's

---

24 Vail, Isaac Newton, *The waters above the firmament*, Publisher Cleveland, O., Clark & Zangerle, 1902, digitized by Google from the library of the New York Public Library

rotation is what accounts for the arctic and antarctic regions of the two poles and the changing of the seasons. According to this theory, the tilting of the earth's axis occurred at the time of the flood. This caused the change in the climate and created the present climate zones. This shift of the earth's axis tilt also brought about much of the violent upheaval that created our current landscape.

It is impossible to know what the exact conditions were that prevailed in the antediluvian world. However, it is possible and even probable that one of these conditions did exist. It is entirely possible that both conditions may have existed together. These conditions would have indeed created a climate that was uniform and mild. The water canopy would explain the healthy environment and explain the enormous amount of rainfall during the Deluge.

CHAPTER 7

The Construction of the Ark

BECAUSE NOAH FOUND FAVOR in the eyes of the Lord, God decided to spare him and his family and some of each species of animals, birds, and reptiles. To accomplish this, God gave Noah instructions for building a huge boat (ark).

> "So make yourself an ark of cypress wood; make rooms in it and coat it with pitch inside and out. This is how you are to build it: The ark is to be three hundred cubits long, fifty cubits wide and thirty cubits high. Make a roof for it, leaving below the roof an opening one cubit high all around. Put a door in the side of the ark and make lower, middle and upper decks." (Genesis 6:14-16)

The ancient cubit was a measurement based on the length of the forearm, from the bottom of the elbow to the tip of the middle finger, of the average person. These ancient cubits ranged in length from 17.5 inches to 24 inches. In the key civilizations like Egypt and Babylon, the cubit had two distinct sizes, a shorter "common" cubit around 18 inches and a longer "royal" cubit of 20 to 21 inches.

Using the length of the common cubit, the Ark would have been 450 feet long, 75 feet wide, and 45 feet high. It was to have three decks with a combined area of 101,250 square feet, and a capacity of over one and a half million cubic feet. It was a vessel of over 43,000 tons, and nearly equal in size to the Titanic. The ark's actual cubic volume and tonnage were not exceeded until the arrival of the oil supertankers.

We do not know which cubit Noah used. Most Biblical writers use the common cubit when referring to the Ark. However it is more likely that Noah used the longer cubit, the same as Solomon did when building the temple. If Noah did use the royal cubit of measurement, then the ark could have been considerably larger at 525 feet long, 87.5 feet wide, and 52.5 feet high.

In 1609 a Holland company built a ship after the pattern of the ark. It revolutionized the shipbuilding industry. Today most ships are still built to similar proportions. There is no way that Noah would have had the knowledge to build the ark, without the divine instructions from God. The vessel that Noah built was very different and much larger than boats of that era.

The Mesopotamian area between the Euphrates and Tigris rivers is believed to have been a densely populated and advanced society in the time of Noah. The boats that the Mesopotamians were building, based on iconographic evidence, were small flat-bottomed boats with high curving ends, with a stem often ending in an elaborate design. These boats were powered by oars or a combination of oars and a fixed sail. They were very limited to the number of people or the amount of cargo that they could carry.[25]

In comparison, the ark that Noah built would be much closer in design and size to the Titanic, than to the boats of his time. Noah's Ark may be the largest wooden ship ever built, with the possible exception of Chinese vessels of Zheng He in the 1400's. It would be quite an engineering project to build such a ship as the Ark, even using today's technology.

In 1993 Dr. Seon Hong headed up a scientific study at the ship research center KRISO, based in Daejeon, South Korea. Dr. Hong's

---

25 Ancient Mesopotamians.com, *Ancient Mesopotamian Ships, Boats for River Transportation*, 2013

team compared twelve hull designs including the ark, as described in Genesis. They discovered that no hull design significantly outperformed the 4,300-year-old design. In fact, it was determined that the Ark could have handled waves as high as one hundred feet.[26]

Only God could have given Noah the knowledge to build such a gigantic vessel in the days before the flood. A boat that would withstand the raging waters of the flood and then the extremely violent waters caused by volcanoes, earthquakes, and upheavals as the mountains and topography of the earth was being changed. The Ark in itself is evidence that it was a global deluge.

---

26 Answers in Genesis, *Safety Investigation of Noah's Ark in a Seaway,* Journal of Creation 8, no. 1, April, 1994.

CHAPTER 8

The Animals in the Ark

SOME OF THE OBJECTIONS to a global flood actually happening, centers upon the animals. For Instance, how did they all fit into the ark? How they all were gathered? And how were they cared for by only eight people?

One of the objections used is that it would have been impossible for animals of different continents to travel to where the ark was. This would seem to be a reasonable view if we were looking at the present world. However, that is not the case. The antediluvian world that existed before the flood was one land mass and would have been much easier to traverse than the world where we now live.

The climate of the antediluvian earth was a uniform warm and moderate climate worldwide. The land was not separated by oceans or impassable mountain ranges. There would have been no limiting factors, such as temperature, climate, elevation, and terrain, to determine where certain animals could exist and others could not. It is not unreasonable, therefore, to assume that animals of all species were scattered throughout the whole earth. In which case, it would not have been necessary for the animals to have to travel from all around the globe to get to the Ark. However, since the construction of the Ark took one hundred and twenty years, there would have been plenty of time for animals to come from any location on the earth if need be.

Nor can we factor out the divine intervention of God in the gathering and bringing together of the correct number and kinds of animals. There is no mention of Noah and his sons gathering the animals. God brought them to the Ark at the right time and then into the Ark.

"*Take with you seven pairs of every kind of clean animal, a male and its mate, and one pair of every kind of unclean animal, a male and its mate, and also seven pairs of every kind of bird, male and female, to keep their various kinds alive throughout the earth.*" (Genesis 7:2-3)

There have been estimates by those who wish to discredit the Biblical flood account, that the number of animals supposedly on the Ark would have been in the millions, and therefore it couldn't have happened. These type of estimates of the number of animals are not only wrong, but they border on the absurd, by people who simply don't know the scriptures or more often just wish to disprove the Flood account.

Notice that the scriptures say "kinds" of animals, not species. For instance, there was two of the dog family, two of the pig family, two of the horse family and so on. In the thousands of years since the flood, the animals that were aboard the Ark could easily have diversified into the varieties that we know today.

There were seven of each of the clean animals. However, there were comparatively few animals that were classified as clean.

There have been more reasonable estimates of the number of animals on the ark ranging from 15,000 to 35,000. Of these, there are very few really large animals, and very young animals could have represented these. It is conceivable that many animals aboard the Ark were young animals. Even if they were all adult animals and they numbered 35,000, there would have been more than adequate space for them.

Naval architects made up a scale model of the Ark and determined that it would certainly be large enough to hold a pair of each kind of animal, bird, and insect we have today, as well as Noah and his family, and a vast food supply.[27]

To care for thousands of animals would have been a daunting task for eight people, even when we consider that the animals were inactive and would require much less food than normal. We have to believe that the omnipotent God had a hand in the care of his creatures. It is possible that they were in a semi-dormant state or a type of hibernation.

---

27 Peter and Paul Labonde, *301 Startling Proofs & Prophecies,* Niagara Falls, Ontario, Prophecy Partners, Inc., 1997

The entire Noachian Flood was a supernatural event, and the gathering and care of the animals were simply part of God's plan.

As for after the flood, the animals of the postdiluvian world found a very different environment concerning climate, weather, terrain, and food supplies. As these animals multiplied and spread out over the earth, they had to adapt to the changed conditions and weather patterns. Different species became distributed in distinct biological and climatic zones. Animals that could not adjust to these new conditions perished and disappeared entirely. Dinosaurs were probably among these.

Were dinosaurs still alive at the time of the flood? It would seem most likely, for how else would you explain the enormous number of dinosaur fossils which only an event like the flood could deposit. We will cover this subject much more in chapter 20. However, one indication that they were still alive involves the degradation of organic protein compounds.

"There's no question, even among some evolutionary naturalists, that unmineralized dinosaur bone still containing bone protein resides in many locations throughout the world. This is amazing, and destroys the mantra of dinosaurs becoming extinct "65 million years ago." Simply put, bone containing such well preserved protein could not possibly have existed for more than a few thousand years in the geological settings in which they are found."[28]

---

28 Frank Sherwin, *Biology and the Age of the Earth,* Institute for Creation Research, 2004

CHAPTER 9

The Duration of the Flood

GENESIS 7:11-12 TELLS US that the windows of heaven were opened and it rained upon the earth for forty days and nights. Verse 19 states that *"the waters prevailed exceedingly upon the earth."* The vast canopy of water above the firmament condensed and poured down upon the earth. This was not a localized rainstorm like we are used to. It was a worldwide torrential rain that continued at full intensity for forty days and nights. We have all seen the effects, on television or in person, of storms that caused flooding and raging rivers that cause massive destruction. Compared to the rain and flooding of God's judgment at the time of Noah, these would seem like trickling little roadside streams. Such intense rain, within hours, would have caused raging rivers. Within days there would have been water hundreds of feet deep and miles wide rushing downward. This swift-moving water would have totally transformed the landscape.

Verse 17 tells that the water began to rise and lifted the ark above the earth as it floated on the surface. Verse 19 says that the waters increased greatly upon the earth, "And the waters prevailed exceedingly upon the earth, and all the high hills under the whole heaven were covered" (NKJV). Not only did it rain hard for forty days and forty nights, but God opened the springs from deep within the earth, and the water poured forth. Verse 12 tells us, *"all of the springs of the great deep burst forth."* It wasn't until 1977 that Bob Ballard discovered the first of many deep ocean springs:

"In 1977, scientists exploring the Galápagos Rift along the mid-ocean ridge in the eastern Pacific noticed a series of temperature spikes in their data. They wondered how deep-ocean temperatures could change so drastically—from near freezing to 400 °C—in such a short distance. The scientists had made a fascinating discovery—deep-sea hydrothermal vents."[29]

In (Genesis 7:24), we read that the water continued coming forth out of the earth for 150 days before God stopped the flow of water (Genesis 8:2). Where did all that water come from that came out of the earth? A recent discovery may answer that question. A recent study reveals that a hidden ocean lies some 400 miles beneath North America. This reservoir likely holds three times more water than all the oceans combined. The discovery was reported on June 12, 2014, in the Journal Science.

New research shows that deep within the Earth's rocky mantle lies oceans' worth of water locked up in a type of mineral called ringwoodite. The Earth's mantle is the hot, rocky layer between the planet's core and crust. Scientists have long suspected that the mantle's so-called transition zone, which sits between the upper and lower mantle layers 255 to 410 miles below Earth's surface, could contain water trapped in rare minerals. However, there has been no direct evidence for this water until now.

"The transition zone can hold a lot of water, and could potentially have the same amount of H2O [water] as all the world's oceans."[30]

God stopped the water flow from within the earth after 150 days, or five months (Genesis 8:2). After which, the water then began to evaporate and form our present atmosphere. Likewise, the water also began to return to deep within the earth.

After a period of seven months and seventeen days, the ark came to rest on the mountains of Ararat (Genesis 8:4). After ten months, the tops of the mountains became visible (Genesis 8:5). After eleven months and twenty-five days, the water had receded from the earth (Genesis 8:5-13). And after twelve months and ten days the earth was dry (Genesis 8:14).

The Biblical record reveals that Noah and his family were on the Ark for a total of one year and ten days. Using the Julian

---

29 National Geographic, *Deep Sea Hydrothermal Vents*, www.education.nationalgeographic.com, 2014

30 LiveScience.com, *Found! Hidden Ocean Locked Deep In Earth's Mantle*, www.livescience.com, 2014

calendar, which has 360 days in a year, would be a total of 370 days. In chapter seven, we read that Noah was six hundred years, one month, and seventeen days old when the flood started. In chapter eight, we see that Noah was six hundred and one years, one month, and twenty-seven days old when he, his family, and the animals embarked from the ark, for a total of one year and ten days. Noah, his family and the animals spent nearly five months on the Ark after it came to rest on the mountain. During this time the waters receded, the mountains appeared, a clean new world appeared and life began anew.

CHAPTER 10

The Depth of the Flood

IN GENESIS, THE BIBLE gives us the depth of the flood:

> "They rose greatly on the earth, and all the high mountains under the entire heavens were covered. The waters rose and covered the mountains to a depth of more than fifteen cubits." (Genesis 7:19-20)

Why did the water cover the mountains by at least fifteen cubits? We find the answer in Genesis 6:15, where we learn that the height of the Ark was thirty cubits Most Bible scholars agree that the "fifteen cubits" refers to the draft of the Ark. The draft was the amount that the ark, would have sunk into the water. In other words, the Ark, when fully loaded, would have sunk into the water to a depth of fifteen cubits, one-half of its overall height.

If the Ark had a draft of fifteen cubits, then the water would have needed to cover the mountains by at least fifteen cubits to keep the ark from striking or grounding on them. How much more than the fifteen cubits, were the mountains covered? That we do not know, but we know that it was upwards of fifteen cubits. With the catastrophic events of the flood, earthquakes, and volcanic action, there would have been enormous waves. Huge waves mean that the water would have needed to be high enough above the mountain peaks so that if the Ark dipped down into a trough (bottom) of a wave, it would not strike the peak.

The implications of the scripture, *"all the high mountains under the entire heavens were covered,"* makes it very clear that this was a worldwide flood. In fact, if only one of the Ararat mountains had been covered, it would have still been a global flood, as water will seek its own level. Geological data seems to indicate that the mountains before the flood were much smaller than present-day mountains.

CHAPTER 11

How the Biblical Account Came About

WE DO NOT KNOW WHAT language was spoken before the flood. It appears that there was a written language and writing taking place before the flood. The Chaldean account of the Deluge stated that Ut-Napishtim, their name for Noah, took written documents called "Tablets of Fate," into the ship with him. The Chaldean account came from legends handed down over time and contained many inaccuracies. Therefore it is an unreliable source. The city of Ur in the Mesopotamia region existed before the Flood. When excavations were done there, they discovered books below the eight to ten feet of flood sediment.

One of the great historians of antiquity was Berosus, a native of Babylonia. Berosus believed that writing was in general use before the flood.

The Jews believe that Enoch, Noah's great-grandfather, left quite a number of writings behind. These may have been taken into the Ark by Noah.

One king of Babylon, whose records were found in the library of Asurbanipal, says that he enjoyed reading the writings produced prior to the era preceding Noah. Archaeologists have found inscriptions that were positively made long before the flood.

The earliest language spoken after the flood that we have knowledge of was known as Akkadian, from Akkad, the northwest section of ancient Babylonia. The Akkadian writing consisted of crossed lines, which eventually developed into the cuneiform writing, about the time of Abraham. The cuneiform writing consisted of wedge-shaped letters and syllables and continued to be in use in Babylonia, Assyria, and Persia, until the time of Christ.

It is believed that when Abrams came to the land of Canaan, at God's command, (Genesis 12:1-5), that he adopted the language of Canaan. This Canaanite language that Abrams utilized or some form of it is believed to have become known as Hebrew.

God called Abrams out of the pagan land of Ur, into the land of Canaan, which he and his descendants were to possess. (Genesis 12:7)

> "Long ago your ancestors........lived beyond the Euphrates River and worshiped other gods. But I took your father Abraham from the land beyond the Euphrates and led him throughout Canaan and gave him many descendants." (Joshua 24:2-3)

In roughly 2000 B.C. God called Abrams, whom he later called Abraham, (Genesis 17:5), to be the head of a people. These people, which God would set apart, would become known as Hebrews or Jews.

> "I will make you into a great nation, and I will bless you: I will make your name great, and you will be a blessing. I will bless those who bless you, and whoever curses you I will curse: and all peoples on earth will be blessed through you." (Genesis 12:2-3)

> "for you are a people holy to the Lord your God. Out of all the peoples on the face of the earth, the Lord has chosen you to be his treasured possession." (Deuteronomy 14: 2)

Dr. J. O. Kinnaman, the great Jewish archaeologist states:
" There is no doubt but that Abraham had, in written form, the traditions and records from Shem, concerning Creation, the Fall of man, the Flood, and God's promises as to the future, for he seems in no wise disconcerted when God instructs him to go " unto a land that I will shew thee."................Abraham himself had a library which he carried into Palestine and Egypt. It was written in the Cuneiform.

How do we know this? We know it from the fact that the part he took to Egypt was left behind and discovered by archaeologists."[31]

About 1500 B.C. God instructed Moses to write down the history of the preceding 2500 years starting with the creation account. It was to include the history of God's people, his laws, promises, prophecies, and the account of Noah and God's judgment upon the earth by the flood. These writings of Moses make up the first five books of the Bible, referred to as the Pentateuch. Since Moses spent considerable time on Mount Sinai in God's presence, I believe that was when he wrote part of the Pentateuch. I can picture this humble man on Mount Sinai, maybe sitting on a big rock, writing as God instructs him. The scriptures themselves make it clear that Moses may have written the words, but the words he wrote were God inspired. There is the phrase "The Lord said to Moses" that is repeated throughout the Pentateuch. Nearly every chapter in Leviticus begins with this phrase. Most of the chapters in Numbers begin this way and many of those in Exodus.

The Scriptures testify to the fact that Moses wrote as God instructed him.

> *"Then the Lord said to Moses, "Write this on a scroll as something to be remembered." (Exodus 17:14*

> *"Moses then wrote down everything the Lord had said." (Exodus 24:4)*

> *"Then the Lord said to Moses, "Write down these words, for in accordance with these words I have made a covenant with you and with Israel." (Exodus 34:17)*

> *"This is the Moses............he received living words to pass on to us." (Acts 7:37-38) (NIV)*

> *"This is that Moses........... the one who received the living oracles to give to us," (Acts 7:37-38) (NKJV)*

The art of writing was around for centuries before Moses wrote down the words of God, especially in Egypt as Dr. Kinnaman wrote:

---

31 J. O. Kinnaman, *Diggers For Facts, Haverhill, MA., Destiny Publishers,* 1945.

"A thousand years before the time of Moses the study of literature, history and religion were professions in Egypt. Everything was recorded; every legal transaction, every commercial act was placed in permanent record. The writing material varied from stone monuments, leather and papyrus, to high-grade vellum."[32]

Undoubtedly there were many earlier documents around before Moses wrote the Pentateuch. While the documents may have been very accurate, we can be sure these were the words and thoughts of man and not from God, simply by the fact that they are no longer around for God's Word remains forever.

"The word of our God endures forever." (Isaiah 40:8)

Critics of the Old Testament have argued that the ancient people of the Old Testament times were too primitive to record documents with precise details. The discovery of the Ebla archive in northern Syria in the 1970's confirmed that the Biblical records concerning the Patriarchs are extremely accurate. It was during these excavations that an extensive library was discovered inside a royal archive room. This library had tablets dating from 2400-2250 BC.

The excavating team discovered about 17,000 ancient tablets. Amazingly, these tablets confirmed that personal and location titles in the Biblical Patriarchal accounts are authentic.[33]

Why did God wait until this time to have his words wrote down? Was Moses someone that God had prepared especially for this task? Who was better qualified than Moses to write these first five books of the Bible, for other than Genesis, his life and works are a big part of these books. Of course, we have no way of knowing the thoughts of God, but we can rest assured that what Moses wrote was indeed the words of the Lord, just as the Scriptures state.

Only the words of God could have endured for thousands of years, unchanged and as relevant today as they were when written.

Other ancient cultures have stories that parallel the biblical account of creation and the flood. Undoubtedly these were handed down within the different cultures from a single ancient source.

---

32 J. O. Kinnaman, *Diggers For Facts*, Haverhill, MA., *Destiny Publishers*, 1945.
33 Clifford Wilson, *Ebla: Its Impact On Bible Records,* Acts and Facts, 6 (4), 1977

The Atrahasis Epic---The Babylonian Genesis: This is the earliest Mesopotamian text with parallels to Genesis. The story, although presented from the theological perspective of the Babylonians, contains many details that are similar to the biblical accounts of the creation and the flood. In the Babylonian tale, the gods rule the heavens and earth. They make man from the clay of earth mixed with blood. When men multiply on the earth and become too noisy, a flood is sent to destroy mankind. One man, Atrahasis, is given a warning of the flood and told to build a boat. He makes a boat and loads it with food and animals and birds. Much of the text is destroyed at this point, so there is no record of the boat's landing. Nevertheless, as in the conclusion of the biblical account, the story ends with Atrahasis offering a sacrifice to the gods.[34]

Enuma Elish--The Mesopotamian Creation: Like the Atrahasis Epic, fragments of this text had also come from Ashurbanipal's library at Nineveh, but other fragments were later found at Ashur and Uruk. Two almost complete tablets were also found at Kish. This tale is a retelling of the creation story from the Babylonian and Assyrian perspective. The universe, in its component parts, began with the principal gods and was completed by Marduk, who became the head of the Babylonian pantheon (assembly of gods).

Parallels with the Genesis account are: the watery chaos is separated into heaven and earth; light pre-exists the creation of sun, moon, and stars; and the number seven figures prominently. Beyond this, however, the mythological context controls the content.[35]

The Chaldean account of the flood: The Chaldean account of the flood was the written account of legends passed down through the centuries. It states that Xisuthrus was visited by a deity and warned that there would be a flood, by which mankind would be destroyed. He was to build a vessel and take his friends and family aboard together with all the different animals and birds.

After the flood had been upon the earth for a time, Xisuthrus sent out birds from the vessel, but not finding any place to land; they returned to him again. After an interval of some days, he sent

---

34 Randall Price, The Stones Cry Out, Eugene, Oregon, Harvest House Publishers, 1997, pp 60,61
35 Randall Price, The Stones Cry Out, Eugene, Oregon, Harvest House Publishers, 1997, pp 61,62

them out a second time, and they now returned with their feet tinged with mud. He sent the birds out a third time, but they did not return. From that, he judged that the surface of the earth had appeared above the waters.

He then made an opening in the vessel, and upon looking out found that it was stranded upon the side of some mountain. They then left the vessel and offered sacrifices to the gods.

The Chaldean account of the flood was the written account of legends passed down through the centuries. There is enough similarity to the Noah flood account, to recognize that it was the same flood. However, the Chaldean flood account had obviously been distorted over time. Thankfully we know that the account God gave to Moses was the accurate one.

The Gilgamesh account of the flood: The Epic of Gilgamesh was discovered in the mid-nineteenth century in the ruins of the great library at Nineveh. Its account of a universal flood has many parallels to the Flood of Noah's day. It is named after King Gilgamesh, who is supposed to have ruled the Mesopotamian city of Uruk around 2600 B.C. The flood story seems to have been borrowed directly from the Atrahasis Epic.

It involved Utnapishtim, a character much like Noah who was told in a dream that there was to be a flood. The flood was in response to man's sin. Utnapishtim was to build a boat and take his family and a few others aboard along with all the different species of animals and birds. It included the releasing of birds as a test for if the flood was over. The boat came to rest upon a mountain.

Dating of the oldest fragments of the Gilgamesh account indicates that it is older than the Genesis account. However, the probability exists that the Biblical account had been preserved either as an oral tradition or even in written form and handed down from Noah, through the patriarchs and eventually to Moses. The Hebrew was known for handing down accurate accounts of events and history. And even if this didn't happen, we know that Moses wrote as God instructed him.

Liberal scholars like to maintain that the Hebrew flood account was borrowed from the Mesopotamian accounts. The differences in religious, ethical, and sheer quantity of details make it extremely unlikely that the Biblical account was dependent in any way on any extant source. Sidney Collett states this quite well:

"The very suggestion that Moses obtained his historical information from those Chaldean and Gilgamesh legends, which Professor Sayce tells us "were traditions before being committed to writing," is simply absurd; for, interesting as they are, they are full of legendary nonsense, that it would have been a practical impossibility for Moses or any other man to evolve, from such mythical legends, the sober, reverent, and scientific records which are found in the book of Genesis."[36]

The many difference between the Mesopotamian and Biblical account are too great for either to have been borrowed from the other. The primary difference being that the biblical account orientation is one God and its characters are ethically moral. By contrast, the Mesopotamian orientation is many gods, and it characters are unpredictable and inconsistent. Many other important details differ greatly. It is much more likely that all accounts originated from the same ancient event.

"It seems more likely that both the Mesopotamian and Israelite accounts reflect a universally preserved knowledge of events that occurred during the earth's pre-Flood history."[37]

"Granted that the Flood took place, knowledge of it must have survived to form the available accounts; while the Babylonians could only conceive of the event in their own polytheistic language, the Hebrews, or their ancestors, understood the action of God in it."[38]

The Hebrew account is more historical and factual in nature, while the Mesopotamians accounts are extremely legendary in character. The tone differs dramatically between the two. The divine inspiration of the Bible demands that the Genesis account is the correct version. While the Mesopotamian accounts do substantiate the Genesis Flood, they in no way predate or replace it as the true flood account.

---

36 Sidney Collett, *All About The Bible,* Westwood, N.J., Barbour And Company, 1989.
37 Randall Price, *The Stones Cry Out*, Eugene, Oregon, Harvest House Publishers, 1997, p70
38 A.R. Millard, *A New Babylonian 'Genesis' Story*, Tyndale Bulletin 18, 1967, p 18

CHAPTER 12

The Biblical Evidence of the flood

IN CHAPTER FIVE OF Genesis we see the lineage of Noah, from Adam to the time of the flood. Chapters six through nine we are given the account of the flood. We are told the reason for the flood, the building of the Ark, the saving of Noah, his family, and the animals, birds, and reptiles. We read of Noah's sacrifice to God and of God's covenant with Noah and his descendants. In chapters nine and ten, we see the lineage of Noah, after the flood.

Chapter one of 1 Chronicles records the lineage from Adam to Abraham, including Noah, his family, and his place in history. Hundreds of years later, the prophet Isaiah speaks of Noah and the judgment of mankind by a worldwide flood (Isaiah 54:9). Job likewise, spoke of the flood (Job 22:15-16).

The flood is spoken of several times In the New Testament. Clearly, the account of Noah and the flood was known and believed by the disciples and others. In the books of Matthew and Luke, Jesus tells about the judgment of mankind by a worldwide flood that covered the earth. Likewise, the writer of Hebrews in chapter eleven speaks of Noah, the building of the Ark, and God's judgment upon the earth by the great flood. And in 1 Peter, chapter three and 2 Peter chapter two, the disciple records the history of Noah and the flood.

Can we believe the Bible when it speaks of Noah and the flood? We know that the Bible is the divine word of God spoken through the writers of the scriptures. There is considerable proof that the Bible is true. In fact, the design of the Ark itself is proof of the authenticity of the Biblical account of the flood. The size of the Ark testifies to the fact that it was a worldwide flood. Why else would such a large vessel be needed?

Those who accept past events as presented in the Bible do so, on good authority. For the Bible is a book of history as well as God's outline for man's salvation. It also contains knowledge about nature, prophecy, medical, sanitation and science. It was knowledge that was thousands of years ahead of its time, proving that the scriptures would have to been God inspired.

For instance, In Genesis, God instructs that male babies are to be circumcised when they are eight days old (Genesis 17:12). Medical science has discovered that this is the day that the coagulating factor in the blood, called prothrombin, is at its peak. This is also when the human body's immune system is at its highest level.

The Bible tells us that God hung the earth in space. And that it hangs on nothing (Job 26:7). It told us that earth is round *(Isaiah 40:22)*. It speaks of the weather and water cycles, the wind patterns, the ocean currents, the earth's rotation, and much more. The Bible told us these things thousands of years before man discovered them, proving that the writings were God given. For who but God could have known these things?

The Bible contains thousands of prophecies concerning events that were fulfilled hundreds and thousands of years later, proving its divine source, for only God can predict the future. In Isaiah, God said He has made know the future to us:

"I am God, and there is no other; I am God, and there is none like me.

I make known the end from the beginning, from ancient times, what is still to come...... What I have said, that I will bring about; what I have planned, that I will do." (Isaiah 46:10-11).

Archaeology has continued to prove the Bible true. Historical scholars claimed there was no proof that King Herod, Pontius Pilate, Nebuchadnezzar, Belshazzar, Hezekiah, Darius, and King David ever existed. But archaeological discoveries in recent years have proved they and many more biblical characters did exist. Archaeology has never proved the Bible false; rather it has substantiated the scriptures. Archaeologists continue to find cities and places mentioned in the Bible, such as in 2004 when they discovered the Siloam Pool where Jesus healed the blind man. And in September of 2015, the biblical city of Sodom was discovered.

Excavations show that the city came to a sudden fiery end, just as portrayed in the Bible. In fact, all archaeology finds have agreed with the historical biblical accounts as recorded in the Bible. There has not been a single artifact or discovery made that would disprove what is written in The Word of God.

Dr. Nelson Glueck, the great Palestinian archaeologist and President of the Hebrew Union College stated:
"As a matter of fact, it may be stated categorically that no archaeological discovery has ever controverted a Biblical reference. Scores of archaeological findings have been made which confirm in clear outline or exact detail historical statements in the Bible."[39]

There is such an enormous amount of evidence proving that the Bible is accurate and God inspired, that it would be foolish to believe otherwise. Therefore, it would likewise be foolish not to believe that the Biblical account of Noah and the flood happened exactly as the scriptures tell us. To reject the Genesis account of the flood also means rejecting the New Testament testimony concerning it, including Christ's. (Luke 17:27)

The Bible, by means of divine revelation provides the only way man can have certain knowledge of the events on earth prior to the time of the keeping of historical records. The Bible provides a framework within which the earth's historic geological data fits into remarkably well.

God left us proof of the flood in the fossils and sediments. These, we will deal with in a later chapter.

---

39 Dr. Nelson Glueck, *Rivers In The Desert: History of Negev*, New York, Farrer, Straus, and Cadahy, 1959.

CHAPTER 13

The Case for a Worldwide Flood

THE BIBLICAL ACCOUNT OF THE flood leaves no doubt about it being a worldwide flood. However, in recent years there have been several books written about the flood being only a localized flood within the Mesopotamia valley. In Genesis, we read that all the mountains under the heavens were covered (Genesis 7:19-20). The mountains were not only covered but remained covered for approximately nine months.

In Genesis 7:4, God said: *"and I will wipe from the face of the earth every living creature I have made."* In the 1656 years since creation, the animals and creatures had ample time to inhabit the entire earth. Therefore only a global flood would accomplish God's purpose.

The primary objective of the flood was to destroy all of humanity with the exception of Noah and his family. This is stated several times in Genesis. *"I will wipe from the face of the earth the human race I have created---for I regret that I have made them," (Genesis 6:7)*. Peter also spoke of it (2 Peter 2:5), as did Christ in (Luke 17:26-27). Nothing less than a worldwide flood, would have accomplished this.

Three times God made the promise that he would never again destroy the earth and all living things by the waters of a flood, (Genesis 8:21; 9:11,15). Obviously, God was referring to a worldwide flood. Otherwise, any time there is a catastrophic flood of any size anywhere in the world; God's promise would be broken. It would have been totally out of character for God to have made such a promise, knowing that it would repeatedly be broken with each flood.

If the flood had not been a global flood, there would obviously have been no need for the Ark. During the 120 years that were required for Noah to build the Ark. Noah and his family could more easily have traveled to an area unaffected by the flood. Likewise, the animals could have simply migrated to land beyond the floodplain. The size and design of the Ark testify to the fact that it was a worldwide flood. Without a lengthy global flood, the Ark would have been unnecessary and pointless. The facts of the Ark alone makes the suggestion that it was a localized flood seem ridiculous.

There are those that believe that the Seine River overflowed several times creating twenty-eight layers of sediment containing fossils. However, these same layers extend throughout Russia, Germany, and England.

This also applies to another layer of rock, known as chalk strata. Chalk strata are a type of limestone formed from sediment containing marine fossils, including huge quantities of shells of marine microorganisms such as foraminifera and coccolithophores. This limestone is a very pure form of limestone, which proves that it was not laid down over millions of years, where contamination would have occurred, but rather was laid down quickly in one event. The chalk strata extend three-quarters of the way around the world. It runs from Australia, through Malaysia, India, Germany, France, England, Belgium, Scotland and Ireland. The white cliffs of Dover are an example of this layer of strata. It also occurs in North America in states such as Alabama, Mississippi, Tennessee, Kansas, and Nebraska. Obviously, these sediment layers were the result of a worldwide flood, rather, than localized flooding.[40]

Another piece of evidence that would substantiate a worldwide flood is what the geologist call "rubble drift and ossiferous fissures" Rubble drift is a certain type of deposit or sediment consisting of massive angular unrolled material tumultuously deposited in local pockets and catchment areas generally full of shattered bones. And by "ossiferous fissures" are meant great fissures or tears in the earth which were formed by some violent action to the surface of the earth. Much of the following information is taken from Alfred M. Rehwinkel book, *The Flood: In the Light of the Bible, Geology, and Archaeology*.[41] Rubble drift is a term

---

40 Andrew A. Snelling, *Can Flood geology explain thick chalk beds?*, Journal of Creation, volume B, issue 1, April 1994.
41 Alfred M. Rehwinkel, *The Flood: In the Light of the Bible, Geology, and Archaeology*. St. Louis, Mo., Concordia Publishing House, 1951

that I was unfamiliar with until I read Mr. Rehwinkel book and Henry Howorth's, *The Mammoth and the Flood*.[42] However, doing research on this, I was unable to find anything written in recent years concerning rubble drift. That could simply be because none has been deposited in the last few thousand years, as this was a one-time occurrence due to the global flood. I expect that any evidence of these has long been destroyed by man's activities.

The evidence for such fissures has been found in many places of the earth, some of them measuring three hundred feet in depth. They are filled with debris which drifted into them soon after they opened. Such fissures have been found in England, France, Spain, Germany, Russia and elsewhere. The interesting feature of these fissures is the debris found in them, for they are filled with the remains of animals, among them are those of the elephant, rhinoceros, hippo, caribou, horse, hog, and oxen. The bone can not be from animals that fell in alive and were buried there, for no skeleton is complete. They cannot have been brought there by streams, for there were no signs of them having been rolled. Neither could they have been exposed to the weather for a long time, for none of the showed signs of weathering. That water had something to do with depositing them is indicated by the general cementing together from the deposits by calcite.[43]

These ossiferous fissures are usually found on isolated hills of considerable height. Places you would expect animals to gather that were seeking safety from an impending flood. Fleeing from the flood waters, the carnivorous and the herbivorous alike sought refuge on the hilltops.

"A classical example of such a fissure s found in Burgundy, France, in the valley of the Soane. The hill is about 1,030 feet above the surrounding plain. A fissure near the top is crowded with animal skeletons. No skeleton is complete, the bones are fractured, thrown together in disorderly fashion, they are not weathered or show no any signs of gnawing on them. Again there is the strange collection of animals that normally do not live together such as bear, horse, wolves, and oxen. They came together seeking safety only to end up together in a watery grave."[44]

---

42 Henry Howorth, *The Mammoth and the Flood*.Whitefish, Montana, Kessinger Publishing, 2010
43 Alfred M. Rehwinkel, *The Flood: In the Light of the Bible, Geology, and Archaeology*. St. Louis, Mo., Concordia Publishing House, 1951
44 Henry Howorth, *The Mammoth and the Flood*.Whitefish, Montana, Kessinger Publishing, 2010

"Here may be found bones of animals by the cartload, and the hard parts and druit of vegetation, both terrestrial and aquatic."[45]

Another example is found in a fissure on the island of Cerigo, off the coast of Greece. This occurs on a barren mountain, referred to as the mountain of bones. It is a mile in circumference at the base, and from the base to the summit is covered with bones. The animals could not have gathered here to feed. The most reasonable solution to this unusual event would be that the animals were driven here ahead of approaching floodwater.[46]

A similar deposit in fissures, some of them, nearly three hundred feet deep were found on the Rock of Gibraltar.

In a large deposit in a cavity near Odessa, Russia, were found 4,500 bones of bears from at least one hundred different animals. Along with these were found the remains of species of the cat family, hyenas, horses, hogs, mammoth, rhinoceros, cattle, and deer, together with the remains of numerous insectivores and rodents such as hares, otters, martens, as well as wolves and fox.[47]

A worldwide flood would seem to be the only logical explanation for such a mixture of animals to assemble on high elevations all over the world. Approaching flood waters could be the only logical reason such a large variety of animals would gather together on these hills.

If there never was a global flood, then why would nearly every culture on earth have their story of it? Although many of these stories became distorted over the centuries, they all share enough similarities to the Biblical account of Noah and the flood, to show that they all originated from a single source. After the flood, as the descendants of Noah became more numerous, they would have moved throughout the earth, forming their own nations and cultures. This would have been especially true after God confused their languages at the Tower of Babel. Those that spoke a common language would have stayed together, eventually forming their own culture. Embedded within this cultural history would have been the story of Noah and a worldwide flood, which would have been past down generation to generation.

---

45 Abbott, WJ Lewis. "The ossiferous fissures in the valley of the Shode, near Ightham, Kent." *Quarterly Journal of the Geological Society* 50.1-4 (1894): 171-187.
46 Alfred M. Rehwinkel, *The Flood: In the Light of the Bible, Geology, and Archaeology.* St. Louis, Mo., Concordia Publishing House, 1951
47 Ibid

CHAPTER 14

The Earth's Strata Deposits

STRATIFICATION (OR LAYERED SEQUENCE) is a universal characteristic of sedimentary rocks. A stratum of sediment is formed by deposition under essentially continuous and uniform hydraulic conditions. When the sedimentation stops for a while before another period of deposition, the new stratum will be visibly distinguishable from the earlier by a stratification line (actually a surface). Distinct strata also result when there is a change in the velocity of flow or other hydraulic characteristics. Sedimentary beds as now found are typically composed of many "strata," and it is in such beds that most fossils are found.

When we see the destruction on television or even in person that a rainfall of six inches or more can cause, it is not hard to realize that a rain of the magnitude spoken of in the scriptures could easily transform the earth's surface. A hard rain of only a few inches can wash out bridges, change river courses and cause millions of dollars in destruction. Can we even comprehend what a deluge of rain that covered the entire earth at the same time and rained hard for forty days and nights would do? We have all seen pictures of massive landslides from the rain-saturated soil. These landslides would have been minor compared to what would have happened with the torrential downpour when the "floodgates of heaven" were opened. If we imaged the very worst flood disaster that our minds could dream up, it probably would not come close to what took place when God opened the sky and the springs deep within the earth.

We have witnessed many disastrous floods in the past, such as the Dayton flood of 1913. An eyewitness to the event wrote:

"No boat could live for a minute in a rushing current which took houses, bridges, railroad tracks and telegraph poles, everything in its overwhelming sweep. I saw the levee which protected the entire west side and which was described as strongly built of gravel, with an average height of twenty-five feet and thirty-five feet broad at the base suddenly melt into the river. The great Pennsylvania four track right of way, part of the finest roadbed in America, melted away like salt. The track on the west side looked like a handful of tangled string thrown into a puddle. One could only get an idea of the strength of the raging flood when the great bridge weighing hundreds of thousands of pounds, floated down stream hundreds of feet before sinking out of sight."[48]

Another eyewitness describing the same flood in Peru, Indiana, wrote:

"We saw the Broadway Bridge go out and the wreckage rush down with the flood against the interurban bridge, a concrete structure. The wreckage was hurled with such force against the concrete pier that it snapped like a matchstick and was lost to view in a swirl of water."[49]

One of the most catastrophic floods in America's history was the Johnstown flood of 1889. An eyewitness of this disaster wrote:

"A solid wall of water forty feet high splurged down the mountain, sweeping everything in its path. Six small villages were practically picked off their foundations and their wreckage hurled with terrific force full upon the people of Johnstown. Few had any chance to escape. They were picked up with their houses and smashed down against the hapless town. The accumulated ruin of eight small villages was carried full force against the stone bridge at the foot of the valley."[50]

The Johnstown flood swept away everything in its path. Houses, buildings of all kinds, trees, railroad cars, animals and people were all thrown together into a great turmoil and swept away. This was a great disaster destroying much property and many lives.

---

48 Logan Marshall, *Our National Calamity of Fire, Flood and Tornado,* L.T.Meyers, 1913, Amazon Indie Digital Publishing
49 Ibid
50 Lowell Thomas, *Hungry Waters, The Story of The Great Flood,* Philadelphia, The John C. Winston Co., 1937

If we were to take these floods and multiply them 100,000 times, we might have an inkling of what the flood of Noah's day was like. These floods were the result of a few days of rain in small areas of the country. Can you image the effect of forty days and nights of a heavy global rain? The steady pounding rain for such an extended time would loosen and soften the soil, turning it into liquid mud. It would be carried into the streams and rivers. These streams and rivers would have soon overflowed and become raging torrents, possibly hundreds of miles wide, carrying billions of tons of soil with them. The unrelenting pounding rain would eventually turn hills and mountains into vast seas of mud and rocks and sediment, which would be carried downstream for hundreds, maybe thousands of miles.

Whole forests and other vegetation would have been carried away in great mats by the floodwater to be buried by mud and sediment as the destructive water rush down to the oceans. These trees and plants would eventually decay and be changed into coal.

There would be layer after layer of mud, silt, sand and rocks laid down as different types of soil and minerals are carried along as sediment by the rush of rivers and flood waters. Sediment layers would form as the current slowed, changed directions, increased, carried different minerals or chemicals, or changed in any number of ways. Consequently, these layers would begin to form into different layers of strata. Later as the waters covering the earth are receding and flowing down to the oceans, they could cut channels and valleys through these layers of soft sediment, exposing the different layers. There is evidence that most rivers were much larger at one time, such as when the waters from the Flood were receding.

The evolutionist claims these different layers each took millions of years of sediment and erosion to create. For instance, if you look at the Grand Canyon you will see that most of the different layers are defined by sharp edges from one layer to the next. The different individual layers do not show the effects of millions of years of erosion upon them as they were slowly formed. If as the evolutionist claim that eons of erosion had been taking place, there would be no definite defining edges. You would easily be able to see the effects of millions of years of erosion on each layer, and from one layer to the next.

Quite often we can view where several layers of strata have gone through upheavals and have been bent or folded upwards. The strata layers are still intact and not broken up. The only way this would be possible is that these upheavals happened while the entire layer were still soft sediment. The photo of the Sullivan River area in British Columbia, show sharp folds in the strata that show no signs of tensile cracking. Obviously, these were formed while the sediment layers were still soft and pliable. Otherwise, instead of bending or folding, these strata layers would just be a jumbled mess of broken rocks.

Another major difficulty of the uniformitarian concept of sedimentary processes is explaining how those great areas of very thick deposits which have gone through one or more cycles of uplift and submergence and yet remain marvelously horizontal and continuous happened.

A good example is found in the Colorado plateaus. This region occupies some 250,000 square miles, including most of Utah and Arizona, with large segments of Colorado and New Mexico. The Grand Canyon and many other spectacular canyons have been excavated through thousands of feet of these flat-lying sedimentary rocks.[51]

---

51 Alfred M. Rehwinkel, *The Flood: In the Light of the Bible, Geology, and Archaeology*. St. Louis, Mo., Concordia Publishing House, 1951

After the flood, there must have been large areas of the earth that were devoid of vegetation and would have remained barren for decades or even centuries, before grass, plants and the trees slowly reclaimed it. During this time the effects wind and weather erosion had on these areas would have been incalculable. Valleys, gorges, lake bottoms would have filled with the dirt and silt being washed away. Massive amounts of soil would have been displaced from the uninterrupted wind. Eventually, all this erosion would solidify into sandstone, shale and clay deposits or other forms of sedimentary rock. This could of have taken place in decades, or possibly centuries rather than the accepted millions of years.

Dr. Henry Morris states: "We shall find not only that there is no type of geologic feature which cannot be explained in terms of rapid formation but that there are in fact a great many such features which can only be explained that way."[52]

Coal and Oil: It is generally accepted among geologists that coal came from ancient plants and oil came from ancient marine animals, including fish. The vast coal beds testify to how lush the vegetation was preceding the flood. Likewise, the enormous oil reserves indicate how plentiful the animals and fish were in the antediluvian world. The puzzling thing to the evolutionist is that there are no oil or coal deposits from before the Cambrian period or after the Pliocene (ice age) period, in other words, these deposits were laid down during the time of the Flood. Neither coal nor oil is being formed today.

"Petroleum occurs in rocks of all ages from the Cambrian to the Pliocene inclusive, but no evidence has been found to prove that any petroleum has been formed since the Pliocene"[53]

"Why did no petroleum form after the Pliocene era? This is a mystery to evolutionary geologists, but it is no problem to Flood geology. From the beginning of the Cambrian to the end of the Pliocene, was when the Flood occurred."[54]

---

52 Morris, Henry M., Scientific Creation, Master Books, El Cajon, Ca. 1985
53 Ben B. Cox, "*Transformation of Organic Material Into Petroleum Under Geological Conditions,*" Bulletin of the American Association of Petroleum Geologists, May 1946, p. 647
54 Evolution Facts Inc., Evolution Encyclopedia Volume 2, *Effects of the flood*, Part 1 Chapter 19

Polystrate fossils: A polystrate fossil is a fossil of a single organism (such as a tree trunk) that extends through more than one geological stratum. This term is typically applied to "fossil forests" of upright fossil tree trunks and stumps that have been found worldwide. Large fossils which extend through several strata layers create a problem for the evolutionist that are claiming that millions of years existed between the different layers of sediment. If each layer took millions of years to accumulate, it would be impossible for a single fossil to extend through three, four or more layers.

"Probably the most widely recognized of the polystrate fossils are tree trunks that extend vertically through two, three, four or more sections of rock—rock that supposedly was deposited during vast epochs of time. However, organic material (like wood) that is exposed to the elements will rot, not fossilize. Thus, the entire length of these

tree trunks must have been preserved very quickly, which suggests that the sedimentary layers surrounding them must have been deposited rapidly—possibly (and likely) during a single catastrophe." [55]

"Polystrate trees are fossil trees that extend through several layers of strata, often twenty feet or more in length. There is no doubt that this type of fossil was formed relatively quickly; otherwise it would have decomposed while waiting for strata to slowly accumulate around it."[56]

In the Craigleith Quarry in England, a tree trunk was found intersecting 10-12 successive strata of limestone.[57] Certainly, the tree could not have grown up through the strata without sunlight and air. The only alternative is a rapid burial. Some polystrate trees are

---

55 Ken Ham, *Did Adam Have A Belly Button*, Green Forest, Ar., Master Books, 2009
56 Scott M. Ruse, *The Collapse of Evolution*, Grand Rapids, Mi. Baker Books, 2011
57 Alfred M. Rehwinkel, *The Flood: In the Light of the Bible, Geology, and Archaeology*. St. Louis, Mo., Concordia Publishing House, 1951

upside down, which could occur in a large flood. Soon after Mount St. Helens erupted in 1980, scientists saw trees being buried in a similar way in the lake-bottom sediments of Spirit Lake. Polystrate tree trunks are found worldwide.

After the explosion of Mount St. Helens on May 18, 1980, Spirit Lake was filled with trees, many of which were floating vertically, due to the weight of their roots. This explains what took place at the time of the Flood, as trees were washed into an area and then covered by a rapid deposit of sediment.

Polystrate tree fossils are proof that the strata layers were deposited along with trees in a single flood, not over billions of years. Once again the Great Flood is the logical time when this would have occurred. The geological data cannot all be explained by evolution and uniformitarianism, but it can be explained by the biblical flood account, as Dr. Austin states below:

"Before radiometric dating was devised, uniformitarian geologists postulated "periods" of millions of years duration to slowly deposit the strata systems. A single sedimentary (layer) lamina, or bed, was supposed by uniformitarian geologists to represent typically a year or many years duration. It was concluded, therefore, that multiplied thousands of laminae and beds superimposed required millions of years. Recently, however, geologists have discovered that laminae and beds form quickly on floodplains of rivers during floods, in shallow marine areas during storms, and in deep water by turbidity currents. The evidence of rapid sedimentation is now so easily recognized that geologists observing a strata system these days often ask where to insert the "missing time" of which the strata do not show sedimentary evidence. Catastrophism, quite naturally, is making a come-back. There is good reason to believe that entire strata systems, and even groups of systems, were accumulated in a hydraulic cataclysm matching the description of Noah's Flood in the Bible."[58]

Varves: A common argument that evolutionist used against the Bible was varves. Varves are rock formations with alternating thin layers of fine dark, and coarse light sediment. It was assumed

---

58 Steven A. Austin, *Ten Misconceptions About the Geologic Column,* Acts & Facts 13 (11), 1984

that these alternating layers represented annual changes with the dark layers being laid down in winter and the light layers in summer. Some formations contain hundred of thousands of varves. The Green River Formation of Wyoming contains more than a million varve pairs in some parts of its formation. These were considered proof that the earth was millions of years old. But the assumption that it took a year for each pair to form has been shown to be wrong. The flood of Noah's day could have deposited these very quickly as more recent catastrophes have shown. One example is the Mount St. Helens eruption that produced twenty-five feet of finely layered sediment in a single afternoon, containing hundreds of alternating layers.

Mount St. Helens Volcano: The eruption of Mount St. Helens in Washington State on May 18, 1980, is one of the most significant geologic events in the United States in the last century. The explosion, on May 18, was initiated by an earthquake and rockslide involving one-half cubic mile of rock. As the summit and north slope slid off the volcano that morning, pressure was released inside the volcano-where super hot liquid water immediately flashed to steam. The northward-directed steam explosion released energy equivalent to 20 million tons of TNT, which toppled 150 square miles of forest in six minutes. In Spirit Lake, north of the volcano, an enormous water wave, initiated by a one-eighth cubic mile of rockslide debris, stripped trees from slopes as high as 850 feet above the pre-eruption water level. The total energy output, on May 18, was equivalent to 400 million tons of TNT-approximately 20,000 Hiroshima-size atomic bombs.

Institute for Creation Research scientists have spent three summers investigating the geologic changes which have occurred at the volcano.

Up to 400 feet thickness of strata has formed since 1980. These deposits include laminae and beds from one millimeter thick to greater than one meter thick, each representing just a few seconds to several minutes of accumulation.

While it is generally claimed that strata layers were accumulated very slowly over long periods of time. The events at Mount St. Helens teach us that the stratified layers which make up the geological formations can form very rapidly.

Erosion has carved a canyon system up to 140 feet deep resembling a small Grand Canyon. The small creeks which flow through the headwaters of the Toutle River today might seem, by present appearances, to have carved these canyons very slowly over hundreds or even thousands of years, except for the fact that the erosion was observed to have occurred rapidly.[59]

The Mount St. Helens eruption provided geologic processes which produced formations within a short time, which geologists might otherwise assume required many thousands of years. While the catastrophic event of the Mount St. Helens Volcano was minor compared with the Noachian Flood and the events associated with it. It does show how easily the earth features, even the Grand Canyon, could have been formed by the Great Flood and all the volcanic and tectonic action associated with it.

"Millions of years of erosion by the Colorado River were once the standard explanation for the formation of the Grand Canyon. Even some evolutionary geologists reject that view today, attributing the Canyon's formation to many catastrophic floods. But their worldview can't accept the single global Flood of Noah's day and its after effects."[60]

---

59 Steve A. Austin, *Mt. St. Helens and Catastrophism,* Acts & Facts. 15 (7), 1986
60 Terry Mortenson, *The Key to the Age of the Earth,* Answers Magazine, Oct. 13, 2008, pp. 62–65

CHAPTER 15

Changes to the earth

THE EARTH AFTER THE flood was a vastly different world than before the flood. Gone was the perfect world with the perfect climate God had created. Peter spoke of this, "By these waters also the world of that time was deluged and destroyed" (II Peter 3:6). In its place was a world whose surface was drastically altered from before. It was a land with a much harsher environment and climate.

There were now high mountain ranges such as the Rockies in North America, the Andes in South America and the Himalayas in Asia. Mountain ranges such as these greatly affected the weather and wind. They essentially divided the continents and land masses into different climatic and biological zones.

"The Alps, the Pyrenees, the Rocky Mountains, and even the Himalayas were all many thousands of feet lower than they are now. This is proved by the fact of…. marine deposits of great thickness, which must of have been formed in rather deep water, being found elevated from ten to sixteen thousand feet above the sea level. As an example…the Dent du Midi in Switzerland, where marine shells…...are found at an elevation of 10,940 feet." [61]

Evidence shows that the oceans are much larger than before the Flood. Before the Flood, there was just one land mass that encompassed roughly half of the earth's surface.

---

61 Alfred Russel Wallace, *The Geographical Distribution of Animals,* London, Macmillan and Company, 1876

According to NOAA, the National Oceanic and Atmospheric Administration, ninety-six percent of the earth's water is contained in the oceans.[62] Where did the additional water come from to cover the earth during the Flood? The Bible tells us that it rained for forty days and forty nights over the whole earth. This was not a normal rain, this was a torrential downpour, for God said he opened the floodgates of heaven (Genesis 7:11-12). If half of the earth's water were in the atmosphere as the scripture seems to indicate (Genesis 1:6-8), it would explain how it could rain so hard for so long, and why only a fraction of that amount of water is in the atmosphere today. And also, it would explain why the oceans are larger now than they were before the Flood.

The present atmosphere is much different than it was before the Flood. In our present atmosphere, if all of the water in the atmosphere rained down at once, it would only cover the globe to a depth of 2.5 centimeters, about 1 inch.[63]

The water cycle on our planet operates in a closed system, that means regardless of the amount of evaporation and rainfall going on in any particular area, the total amount of water on the face of the earth never changes.

"Whatever the source of the Deluge rain, the mass of waters which descended to the earth could hardly have been elevated back into the heavens, because it is not there now. This can only mean that much of the waters of our present oceans entered the oceans at the time of the Flood." [64]

Genesis 7:12 states: *"all of the springs of the great deep burst forth."* Genesis 7:24, tells us that the water continued coming forth out of the earth for 150 days, before God stopped the flow of water (Genesis 8:2).

The first deep-sea springs were discovered in 1977.[65] But how could these springs keep flowing for 150 days? We finally have the answer. In June 2014 it was discovered that there is a reservoir of water, larger than

---

62 National Oceanic and Atmospheric Administration, *How much water is in the ocean,* http://oceanservice.noaa.gov/facts/oceanwater.html, 2014

63 U.S.Geological Survey, *The Water Cycle: Water Storage in the Atmosphere,* http://water.usgs.gov/edu, 2014

64 John C. Whitcomb and Henry M. Morris, The Genesis Flood, Phillipsburg, N.J., Presbyterian And Reformed Publishing Co., 1989

65 National Geographic, *Deep Sea Hydrothermal Vents,* www.education.nationalgeographic.com, 2014

all the oceans put together, 400 miles below the earth's surface.[66]

It is easy to visualize the effects upon the earth that, such a huge amount of water coming to the surface might have. The movement of tectonic plates would have caused earthquakes and volcanoes. The great upheavals as mountains and mountain ranges were created where none existed before, and great basins and troughs were opened up in the ocean depths to receive all the water that prior to the flood was in the atmosphere. (Psalms 104:7-8) The forces of nature during the year of the flood were of such enormous magnitude that the human imagination is incapable of comprehending all the catastrophic events. The greatest forces of nature in water, volcanoes, and earthquakes would have made profound geological and hydrological changes which totally reshaped the face of the earth.

The rivers flowing out to the sea would have been much larger as water from the flood receded. Today this is evident by the abundance of small streams and rivers flowing between steep, high sides of large canyons. The flat bottoms of these canyons, called floodplains, sometimes extend considerable distances on either side of many rivers. There are enormous floodplains on both sides of the Mississippi; which extends for many miles. In ancient times, the Mississippi was part of a gigantic river, now referred to as the "Teays River."

"We consistently find valleys with small streams in their center, with evidence that once a very large river coursed down the center of the valley." [67]

"Valleys commonly appear to be far too large to have been formed by the streams that utilize them." [68]

The receding water rushing back to the newly created ocean basins and troughs in great torrential rivers across the newly deposited sediment materials, which had not yet solidified, could easily have gouged out the Grand Canyon, and other canyons and gorges in a matter of days or weeks, instead of the supposed millions

---

66 LiveScience.com, *Found! Hidden Ocean Locked Deep In Earth's Mantle*, www.livescience.com, 2014
67 Evolution Facts inc., Evolution Encyclopedia Volume 2, *Effects of the flood*, Chapter 19, Part 2
68 O.D. von Engeln and K.E. Caster, *Geology*, New York, McGraw-Hill,1952,pp. 256-257.

of years. The receding waters would have carried vast quantities of soil and sediment with them. The Mississippi River, flowing several miles wide, could have easily laid down the thousands of square miles of the Mississippi Delta.

Dr. Graebner tells an amusing story in *God and the Cosmos*, about the alleged time required to lay down the delta deposit of the Mississippi is. It appears that some human remains had been discovered deep down in the delta deposit near New Orleans, Louisiana. The age of these remains was estimated at 57,000 years, but a short time later a piece of wood at Port Jackson was found at a still greater depth, and an examination of this wood proved it to be from the gunwale of a Kentucky flatboat. The impressive 57,000 years thus shriveled to a modest 200 years or less.[69]

The end of the flood did not mark the end of geological changes to the earth. A much larger portion of the earth's surface was now being taken up by water. There was the creation of great mountain chains, huge valleys, and deep ocean basins. All of these would have greatly altered the earth's surface. The removal of the vapor canopy would have instituted a whole new hydrologic system with seasons, drastic climate changes, new water and wind cycles. The extreme cold at the north and south poles was a new thing. All of these things in addition to all the tectonic movement, earthquakes etc. would have vastly altered the earth. The settling and adjusting to these new conditions would have continued for many years or even centuries.

"All the great mountain ranges of the present world came into existence during this period. The fossils found in the strata are an undistributed proof that they came into existence long after they had appeared on earth, and the fact that fossils of marine and land organisms are often found closely associated is evidence that their substance was laid down in a great flood of water." [70]

There are large inland basins where water remained after the flood for possibly centuries or more. In Asia, in western North America, in northern Africa, and in Australia there are large interior basins without any drainage to the oceans. The physical evidence points to the fact that these basins were full of water at one time. One of these named Lake Agassiz covered an area within

---

69 Alfred M. Rehwinkel, *The Flood: In the Light of the Bible, Geology, and Archaeology*, St. Louis, Mo., Concordia Publishing House, 1951
70 Ibid

the present territory of Manitoba, Saskatchewan, Ontario, North Dakota, and Minnesota. An area six hundred and fifty miles long, by two hundred miles wide and five hundred feet deep. The lake was also fed by melting glaciers as they receded at the end of the ice age. Geologists still have questions about its origin and its disappearance. The present Lake Winnipegosis and Lake Winnipeg are remnants of that lake.[71]

Another area of water occupied the greater part of Nevada, Utah, Idaho, Oregon, and California. The Salt Lake in Utah is but a remnant of a much larger body of water, Lake Bonneville. At its greatest extent Lake Bonneville, was approximately 325 miles long and 135 miles wide and its deepest point was over 1000 feet deep. The high water marks are evident on the surrounding mountains.[72]

There are high water marks in the form of raised beaches and terraces formed by ancient lakes found all over the world.

After the flood, it would have been many years, maybe centuries before all the water drained from these inland water basins into the oceans, filling them to current levels. This is evident by the hundreds of the world's rivers that have riverbeds, called canyons; that extend far out into the oceans. They are cut into the continental slope and extend under water even onto the continental shelf. The largest river canyon, extending from the Congo River, is 497 miles long. The Hudson River canyon extends 400 miles out into the ocean.[73] Also, there are a large number of shorter riverbeds that begin underwater along the ocean's coastline, and extend out into the ocean. They are much more numerous on the steeper slopes than they are on, the more gentle slopes, which would be in keeping with the normal pattern of streams and rivers. These river canyons, sometimes called submarine canyons, would seem to prove that the oceans were much smaller at one time. Swift moving water would have been required to cut these river channels before they were submerged under the present oceans. Currents measured in these underwater canyons are usually less than one mile per hours, far too slow to have any river cutting ability.

---

71 Wikipedia, *Lake Agassiz*, http://en.wikipedia.org/wiki/Lake_Agassiz, 2015
72 Amanda Briney, Geography.About.com, *The Great Salt Lake and Ancient Lake Bonneville*, 2015
73 Wikipedia, *Submarine Canyons*, http://en.wikipedia.org/wiki/Submarine_canyon, 2015

More proof of lower ocean levels, are seamounts. Seamounts were first discovered by a naval captain during World War II. While on trips back and forth across the Pacific, Harry H. Hess, commander of an attack transport, the U.S.S. *Cape Johnson,* kept his deep-water echo sounder turned on all the time. Continuous profiles of the sea bottom were recorded on graph paper. Analyzing the data, he discovered extinct volcanoes hundreds of feet beneath the sea with their tops flatten off. None of them broke the surface of the ocean. Seamounts are the result of volcanoes in the basin of the ocean which became extinct before the seas had filled. Their summits were eroded away and flattened out by storm and wave action at the surface of the ocean at that time. The oceans kept filling, and the horizontal tops became submerged hundreds of feet below the surface.[74]

The continental shelves that surround all the continents on the globe are yet another evidence of a lower sea level at some earlier time. These shelves extend an average of forty-two miles out into the ocean. However, some extend as far as seven hundred and fifty miles offshore. The outer edge of these shelves appears to mark the level of the ocean, before the oceans filled to their current levels.[75]

The natural processes of today are incapable of producing the great salt, coal, chalk, and gypsum deposits of the past. Nor, are the rivers and waterways capable of laying down continent-wide layers of sediments as were done in the Flood. Today's rivers could never carve out the deep canyons through the layers of sediment. Modern volcanoes are incapable of producing the enormous lava deposits of the past. And the earthquakes and tectonic action going on today could never create the mountain ranges as were done at the end of the great deluge. The present is not the key to understanding the past. Uniformitarianism does not have the answers to confidently explain the past. Only the catastrophic events associated with a global flood can account for the geological features of the present earth.

"Some form of catastrophism is clearly indicated by the vast evidences of volcanism, diastrophism, glaciation, coal and mineral

---

74 Evolution Facts inc., Evolution Encyclopedia Volume 2, *Effects of the flood,* Chapter 19, Part 2

75 Evolution Facts inc., Evolution Encyclopedia Volume 2, *Effects of the flood,* Chapter 19, Part 2

deposits, fossilization, vast beds of sediments, and most of the other dominant features of the earth's crust. When this fact is once recognized, it can then be seen that even the supposed evidences of the great geologic age can be reinterpreted to correlate well with the much more impelling evidences of violent and rapid activity and formation." [76]

"The earthquakes of the present day are certainly but a faint reminiscence of those telluric movements to which the structure of almost every mountain range bears witness.......great geological processes of episodic disturbances of such indescribable and overpowering violence that the imagination refuses to follow the understanding and to complete the picture of which the outlines are furnished by observation of facts. Such catastrophic have not occurred since the existence of man, at least not since the time of written records." [77]

"Earth has many features which scientist with evolutionary presuppositions cannot explain. But these features can be explained by a gigantic flood, the most cataclysmic and literally earthshaking event the world has ever experienced…." [78]

Ironically, NASA scientists accept that there have been "catastrophic floods" on Mars[79] that carved out canyons[80] although no liquid water is present today. But they deny that a global flood happened on earth, where there is enough water to cover the whole planet to a depth of 1.7 miles if it were completely uniform, and even now covers seventy-one percent of the earth's surface. If it weren't for the fact that the Bible teaches it, they probably wouldn't have any problem with a global flood on earth.[81]

---

[76] John C. Whitcomb and Henry M. Morris, *The Genesis Flood*, Phillipsburg, N.J., Presbyterian And Reformed Publishing Co., 1989

[77] Eduard Suess, *Face of the Earth, cited by,* Price, George McCready, *Illogical Geology,* Rochester, N.Y., Scholar's Choice, 2015

[78] Walt Brown, *In the Beginning: compelling Evidence for Creation and the Flood,* Center for Scientific Creation, Phoenix, Az. 2001, p. 29

[79] R.A. Kerr, *Pathfinder Tells a Geologic Tale with One Starring Role,* Science, 09 Jan 1998: Vol. 279, Issue 5348,

[80] O. Morten, *Flatlands,* New Scientist, 159(2143), July, 1998

[81] Jonathan Sarfati, *Refuting Evolution,* Green Forest Ar., Master Books, 2002

Chapter 16

The Bible vs Evolution and Naturalistic Geology

WELL INTO THE NINETEENTH century most scientist and theologians alike taught that the geological features of the earth were a result of the Noachian Flood. That the flood was worldwide and responsible for the geological changes to the earth was almost universally accepted.

Historian Charles Gillispie wrote; "There was no question about the historical reality of the flood. When the history of the earth began to be considered geologically, it was simply assumed that a universal deluge must have wrought vast changes and that it had been a primary agent in forming the present surface of the globe. Its occurrence was evidence that the Lord was a governor as well as a creator." [82]

It wasn't until Lydell's theory of uniformitarianism that mankind began to look elsewhere than the Bible for their geological answers. This should not surprise us, with Satan's influence; man has always tried to replace God and his Word with his own self-importance and limited knowledge. Man's idea of his self-development, progress, and growth, appeals to his sense of pride and ambition. Hence, the concept of evolution fits into this same line of thought. The truth of the evolutionary theory depends on the non-existence of God. Evolution leaves no room for an omnipotent Creator. Nor can a personal God that is involved in our daily lives fit into the concept of evolution.

The teaching of evolution got a shot in the arm in 1958. The Soviet Union had launched the Sputnik satellite into space, and there was a growing sense that the United States scientists were falling

---

82 Charles C. Gillispie, *Genesis and Geology,* Cambridge, Harvard University Press, 1951.

behind the scientists in the Soviet Union. President Dwight D. Eisenhower and Congress passed the National Defense Education Act, a funding bill designed to improve science education. There were new textbooks, authored by scientists and teaching evolution.[83] "a new uniform set of biology textbooks, whose publication and dissemination were underwritten by the National Science Foundation. An extensive and successful public relations campaign was undertaken to have these books adopted, and suddenly Darwinian evolution was being taught to children everywhere. The elite culture was now extending its domination by attacking the control that families had maintained over the ideological formation of their children." [84]

What we see today is the fulfillment of Bible prophecy that in the last days there will a new philosophy that will lead men to no longer believe in the Flood and God's judgment of mankind (2 Peter 3:3-6). We see the fulfillment of this prophecy in the form of evolutionary uniformitarianism.

Uniformitarianism-The belief that the same natural laws and processes that operate in nature now have always operated in the same order and manner since time began. Therefore, these processes can be measured and the same measurements can then be applied far back into the past or even into the future and will apply everywhere in the universe.

Science can only deal with things that exist in the present. The scientific method relies on being able to measure present material processes. Their belief that the measurements of today's natural processes can be used indefinitely in the past or the future is unproven and can not be proven, since measurement of the prehistoric past or distant future can not be done. When men attempt to interpret the prehistoric past or the distant future, they must leave the realm of true science and enter the realm of guesswork. To determine the age of prehistoric rocks, fossils, etc. using the scientific measurements of today for these changes and assume them to be correct, is not true science as Dr. Morris states:

---

83 Stephanie Pappas, *5 Battles in the War Between Creationism and Evolution,* www.livescience.com, February 4, 2014

84 Richard Lewontin, Review of the Demon-Haunted World, by Carl Sagan. In New York Review of Books, January 9, 1997.

"By projecting the present rates of change into the extreme past, he can develop theories about the evolution of the earth's geology and geography, and life itself. There is nothing off limits, nothing on the earth or in the farthest galaxies, if he desires, for no one can prove him wrong for the simple reason that these events are not reproducible and therefore not subject to scientific checking. It is truly amazing how anything, under the banter of science, is acceptable as fact by a large segment of the populace." [85]

Uniformity and the measurement of the material processes cannot be applied for much of our history. Their belief that all things have continued the same from the beginning of time simply is not true.

For instance, the creation process would have been very different. It was a process that lasted only six days. After this, there would have been no need for more creation. Creation was done, and God had declared it very good, (Genesis 1:31).

After creation, there was a time when life on earth was as God had intended it. It was a time when neither creation nor decay was in process. It was the perfect world God had created for man.

The next time when the natural processes would change would be after Adam sinned and man and the earth were placed under the curse (Genesis 3:17). This would have been the antediluvian period, a time when much of the earth was still the perfect world that God had created for man. But now everything was under the curse. Man, the earth, and the entire universe would have an ending. Now there was a process of aging, running down and decay involved as part of the natural processes.

And of course next there would have been the Deluge itself, a time when the entire geology and climate of the earth was changed drastically.

All of these time periods would have been much different from today's natural processes. Therefore, using measurements of today's natural processes and trying to apply them to the distant past cannot possibly result in the correct conclusions.

"Antediluvian meteorological conditions were quite different in character from those now prevailing. Otherwise, it would have been quite impossible for rain to have fallen continuously for forty days

---

85 Henry M. Morris, *Studies In The Bible And Science,* Philadelphia, PA., Presbyterian and Reformed Publishing Co., 1966.

and forty nights all around the world, especially in such torrential fashion that it was described as the "flood-gates" of heaven being opened. The tremendous amounts of water implied are not possible under present atmospheric conditions. Other evidences of pre-Deluge climatological differences from the present include the references to the early non-existence of rainfall (Genesis 2:5-6); the "water above the firmament" (not "in the firmament"), therefore not the clouds (Genesis 1:7); and the postdiluvian introduction of the rainbow (Genesis 9:13). These conditions described in the Bible add weight to the evidence that the principle of uniformity cannot be applied to the Deluge or to the antediluvian period." [86]

"The idea that the rates or intensities of geological processes have been constant is so obviously contrary to the evidence that one can only wonder at its persistence." [87]

Science is simply the knowledge of principles, from which scientific laws are based. One such law asserts that cold contracts and heat expands. Based on this law when water cools and turns to ice it would contract and become heavier. Thereby, being heavier than water it would sink to the bottom and be replaced at the top by more water, which would start the freezing process all over again until all the water had been turned into solid ice. Based on this particular law, the results would be perfectly logical, due to the assumption that a given law once in process must continue. However, because of God's grand design, just before water reaches the freezing point, it ceases to contract and begins to expand, thereby becoming lighter than the water beneath it, and hence it floats rather than sinks. The Biblical record should not be dismissed or discounted simply because of scientific difficulties in dealing with a particular situation or circumstance such as the global flood.

"What is popularly called science is frequently nothing more nor less than certain theories and conclusions based upon man's limited and imperfect knowledge of God's perfect laws." [88]

---

86 Henry M. Morris, *Studies In The Bible And Science,* Philadelphia, PA., Presbyterian and Reformed Publishing Co., 1966.
87 James H. Shea, "Twelve Fallacies of Uniformitarianism," in Geology, September 1982, p. 457.
88 Sidney Collett, *All About The Bible,* Westwood, N.J., Barbour And Company, 1989.

Even Mark Twain had something to say about science.

"There is something fascinating about science. One gets such wholesale returns of conjectures out such a trifling investment of facts." [89]

Do the Bible and science agree? Let me ask the question another way. Does the perfect Word of God agree with the imperfect knowledge of man? Of course not, for to do so would prove the scriptures to be inaccurate. Much of what was considered scientific knowledge a few hundred years ago has been replaced with newer thinking as man learns. If the Bible had agreed with the scientific thinking of two hundred years ago, that has since changed; it would have obviously been in error. Hence, the same situation exists today. Man's science of today is not perfect. Therefore it is not in perfect agreement with the Bible.

Charles Lyell excited the world with a piece of pottery from under the mud in the Delta of the Nile. By measuring the amount of sediment above it, Lydell determined that the piece of pottery was some thirty thousand years old. This was considered a great triumph of science, and it excited much interest as it was displayed throughout Europe. However, when it was taken to Rome, it was recognized as a piece of somewhat modern Roman pottery.[90] Today this is seen as a colossal blunder. However, it was the "science" of the day, and needless to say, the Bible did not agree with it.

In 1906, an African pygmy was displayed at the Bronx Zoo, as a transitional species between man and ape. Was that the science of the day? [91]

The Bible which throughout time has remained unchanged and as the divine word of God is unchangeable, does not, and can not agree with every scientific theory since the world began. Science is always changing as man's knowledge increases. Only if man's knowledge would become perfect, would the Bible and science be in complete agreement. Science and the Bible are not opposites. As man's scientific knowledge increases, it tends to draw closer to the biblical scriptures.

---

89 Mark Twain, *Life on the Mississippi,* Amazon Digital Services LLC, 2012
90 John C. Whitcomb and Henry M. Morris, *The Genesis Flood,* Phillipsburg, N.J., Presbyterian And Reformed Publishing Co., 1989
91 The New York Times, Mitch Keller, *The Scandal at the Zoo,* August 6, 2006

An example of science moving closer to the Bible comes from Peter and Paul Lalonde:
"For centuries scientists argued that the universe was infinite and eternal. If so, many claimed, there was no beginning and hence nothing for a creator to do. But, we now know that the amount of usable energy in the universe is decreasing. And, scientists agree, if the universe is running down, it cannot be eternal, or infinite. It will have an end just as it had a beginning. Scientists know this principle as the second law of thermodynamics. It is fascinating to know that science's two most foundational discoveries argue for creation, not against it!" [92]

"Whenever a biblical passage deals either with a broad scientific principle or with some particular item of scientific data, it will inevitably be found on careful study to be fully accurate in its scientific insights. Often it will be found even to have anticipated scientific discoveries. The Bible is indeed a book of science, as well as a book of history, literature, psychology, economics, law, education, and every other field." [93]

Historian and philosopher of science Stephen Meyer stated:
"We have not yet encountered any good in principle reason to exclude design (creation) from science. Design seems just as scientific (or unscientific) as its evolutionary competitors.......one might quite legitimately say that both design and decent (evolution) are both historically scientific research programs, since they instantiate the same pattern of inquiry." [94]

The Big Bang theory is man's effort to explain what happened at the very beginning of our universe. Discoveries in astronomy and physics have shown beyond a reasonable doubt that our universe did, in fact, have a beginning. Before that moment there was nothing; during and after that moment there was something: our universe.

Three British astrophysicists, Steven Hawking, George Ellis, and Roger Penrose, done extensive research on Einstein's Theory

---

[92] Peter and Paul Lalonde, 301 startling proofs & prophecies, Niagara Falls, Ontario, Prophecy Partners, Inc., 1997

[93] Henry M. Morris, *The Biblical Basis for Modern Science*, Green Forest, Ar., Master Books, 2002

[94] J.P.Moreland, *The Creation Hypothesis: Scientific Evidence for an intelligent designer*, Downers Grove, Il, InterVarsity Press, 2016, p.98-99

of Relativity. They expanded on his work to include measurements of time and space. According to their calculations, time and space had a finite beginning that corresponded to the origin of matter and energy. While they are not going to admit that the world was created by God, in essence, that is the only logical conclusion to the results of their study.

Their conclusion:
"nothing existed, not space, time, matter, or energy- nothing.......We don't know. We don't know where it (the universe), came from, why it's here, or even where it is. All we really know is that we are inside of it and at one time it didn't exist and neither did we." [95]

As Christians, we know how the universe originated. We understand why it's here and why we are here. The Bible has the answers. Evolution does not, it has theories that cannot be proven and at times are not even logical.

One problem that evolutionists face and one that they can not offer an explanation for is that evolution goes against the proven laws of physical science. The physical processes of the universe all fall into two fundamental laws of science, The First and Second Laws of Thermodynamics. Henry Morris and Martin Clark explain this in their book, *The Bible Has The Answer*.[96] All physical processes deal with energy and the interchanges of it. Even matter itself is a type of energy that under the right conditions can be converted into other forms.

The First Law is the Law of Conservation, which states that nothing is being created or destroyed. We see this Law displayed in the scriptures. Exodus 20:11 tells that after the six days of creation, God rested on the seventh. The creation process was done. All of *"his works had been finished since the creation of the world"* (Hebrews 4:3). He is now *"sustaining all things by his powerful Word"* (Hebrews 1:3). God is no longer creating anything, nor is he allowing anything to be destroyed. It is a proven scientific fact that matter and energy can be changed, however, like the Bible states; it cannot be created or destroyed.

---

95 All About Science, *Big Bang Theory - An Overview,* http://www.allaboutscience.org/big-bang-theory.htm, 2015
96 Henry Morris and Martin Clark, *The Bible Has The Answers, Green Forest, Ar., Master Books,* 2005

The Second Law is the Law of Energy Decay, states that in all natural processes there is a net loss of energy, which results in entropy and decay. It declares that any system left to itself will become disordered and eventually run down and die. We see this process begin after the fall of man,

"Cursed is the ground because of you" (Genesis 3:17).

"They (heaven and earth) will perish, but you remain; they will all wear out like a garment" (Hebrew 1:11).

"The earth will wear out like a garment" (Isaiah 51:6).

Everything in the universe is wearing out. It is an accepted scientific fact, yet evolutionists claim just the opposite. They maintain that man, the animals, and the plants are all evolving into better and more advanced models of themselves. They consider a fundamental principle of evolution, is the continual development and increasing order and complexity throughout the universe. According to "science" that is not taking place and under current conditions, it is impossible, since the current processes of nature are processes of conservation and decay. Evolution is in direct conflict with these proven scientific truths, whereas, creation and the Bible are in direct alignment with these laws.

"No exception to the second law of thermodynamics has ever been found--not even a tiny one." [97]

If we are evolving, where is the proof? Why are we not seeing new species of plants and animals? Mankind has been witness to the extinction of millions of both. Shouldn't new species be evolving at least as fast as others are becoming extinct?

"We are surely losing one or more species a day right now out of the five million on Earth." [98]

"It is significant that not one new species of plant or animal is known to have evolved on Earth during recorded history, but large numbers have become extinct." [99]

---

97 E. H. Lieb and Jakob Yngvason, "A Fresh Look at Entropy and the Second Law of Thermodynamics," Physics Today (vol. 53, April 2000), p. 32.
98 Norman Myers, *The End of the Lines*, Natural History, Vol. 94, Feb. 1985, p 2
99 Henry M. Morris, Scientific Creation, Master Books, El Cajon, Ca. 1985

With the billions of fossils, shouldn't there be transition fossils as species evolved? If evolution is true, scientists should be able to trace the evolution of plants and animals through the fossil record which is the main criteria for their evolution theory. In actuality, the fossil record proves that there has been no evolving whatsoever. Scientists are well aware of this fact, as paleontologist George Simpson admits:

"It remains true, as every paleontologist knows, that most new species, genera, and families, and that nearly all categories above the level of families, appear in the record suddenly, and are not led up to by known, gradual, completely continuous transitional sequences." [100]

While Simpson was speaking mainly of the fossil record of animals, the same is true of plant fossils as paleobotanist C.A. Arnold alludes to:

"It has long been hoped that extinct plants will ultimately reveal some of the stages through which existing groups have passed during the course of development, but it must be freely admitted that this aspiration has been fulfilled to a very slight extent………..As yet we have not been able to trace the phylogenetic history of a single group of modern plants from its beginning to the present." [101]

The Sauropod family of dinosaurs is another example of many problems that the evolutionist faces. Here you have creatures weighing as much as one hundred tons that lived on the earth and then disappeared. How do you claim a one hundred ton animal evolved, when the fossil record shows that there was absolutely no creature ever having lived that the Sauropods could have evolved from beforehand.

Evolutionists also claim birds evolved from reptiles. That is quite a jump from one species to the next. To go from a ground crawling creature, to a marvelous flying creature with a completely different DNA and no real evidence of any transitional form in between. Where is the proof of such a jump in evolution?

Evolutionists claim that Archaeopteryx is a featured dinosaur that was a transition between reptiles and birds. Of the few Archaeopteryx fossils, at least two of them have proven to be forgeries. Apparently, a

---

100 George Gaylord Simpson, *The Major Features of Evolution,* New York, Columbia University Press, 1953
101 C.A. Arnold, *An Introduction to Paleobotany,* cited in Henry M. Morris, *Studies in the Bible and Science,* PA., Presbyterian and Reformed Publishing Co., 1966.

thin layer of cement was spread on a fossil of a chicken-size dinosaur, called Compsognathus. Bird feathers were then imprinted into the wet cement.[102]

For such a great transition, from dinosaur to bird, there should have been enormous numbers of fossils with scales turning into feathers and forelimbs turning into wings. If millions of years were required for this transition, where are the millions of fossils documenting it? There are none as evolutionist William Swinton admits, although he still believes it took place:

"The origin of birds is largely a matter of deduction. There is no fossil evidence of the stages through which the remarkable change from reptile to bird was achieved." [103]

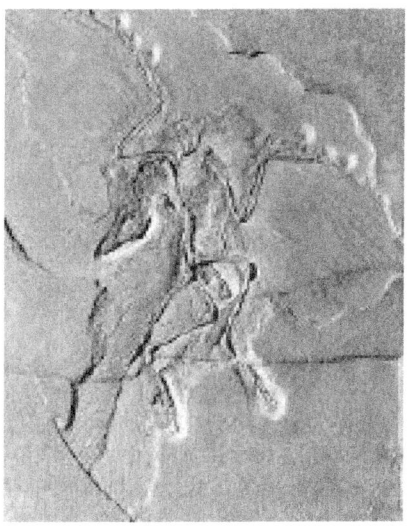

Evolutionist Alan Feduccia, a world authority on birds at the University of North Carolina, says: "It's biophysically impossible to evolve flight from such large bipeds with foreshortened forelimbs and heavy, balancing tails"—exactly the wrong anatomy for flight……..In my opinion, the theropod (Archaeopteryx) origin of birds will be the greatest embarrassment of paleontology in the 20th century." [104]

---

102 Fred Hoyle and N. Chandra Wickramasinghe, *Archaeopteryx, the Primordial Bird: A Case of Fossil Forgery*, Swansea, England, Christopher Davies, Ltd., 1986

103 W.E. Swinton, *Biology and Comparative Physiology of bird*, A.J. Marshall, Ed., New York, Academic Press, 1960, Vol. 1, p.1, quoted from Henry Morris, *Scientific Creationism*

104 Feduccia, Alan. *The origin and evolution of birds*. Yale University Press, 1999.

Feduccia proclaimed: "Paleontologists have tried to turn *Archaeopteryx* into an earth-bound, feathered dinosaur. But it's not. It is a bird, a perching bird. And no amount of 'paleobabble' is going to change that." [105]

University of Kansas paleontologist Larry Martin speaking about two fossils found in China, which were being claimed to be featured theropods, stated:
"You have to put this in perspective. To the people who wrote the paper, the chicken would be a featured dinosaur." [106]

"As further proof that Archaeopteryx is not a transition species, fossils of two modern birds have recently been found in rock strata, dated by evolutionists, as being much older than Archaeopteryx." [107]

Undoubtedly, Archaeopteryx will continue to be proclaimed as a "missing link," as it is the only possible solution to the question of how birds evolved. Given that Archaeopteryx is a mainstay in biology textbooks, students will continue to be misled by this fallacious claim.

"In that great window to the past--the fossil record--we only find distinct plant and animal kinds, with no transitional forms. With the exception of creatures that have become extinct.... ALL life forms found in the fossils are just like those presently alive! To say it again: All non-extinct plant and animal fossils are the same as creatures now alive on the earth. There is NO evidence of evolution in the fossils." [108]

The theory of evolution demands evidence of fossils of transitional specimens, the missing links. Yet, there are absolutely no transitional specimens to be found anywhere. Most astonishing is the fact that Darwin, himself, wrote about this.

"Why if species have descended from other species by fine gradations do we not see everywhere innumerable transitional forms?....why do we not find them embedded in countless numbers

---

105 Alan Feduccia, cited by Joe White and Nicholas Comninellis, *Darwin's Demise*, Green Forest, Ar., Master Books, 2001
106 "Yet another new 'feathered' dinosaur? - creation.com." 2009. 12 Mar. 2016, http://creation.com/yet-another-new-feathered-dinosaur
107 Tim Beardsley, *Fossil Bird Shakes Evolutionary Hypotheses, Nature,* Vol. 322, 21 August 1986
108 Evolution-Facts.org, *Effects of The Flood,* Evolution Encyclopedia Vol. 2, Part 1

in the crust of the earth?....why do we not now find closely-linking intermediate varieties? This difficulty for a long time quite confounded me…... Why then is not every geological formation and every stratum full of such intermediate links? Geology assuredly does not reveal any such finely graduated organic chain; and this, perhaps, is the most obvious and gravest objection which can be urged against my theory." [109]

Not only is there no evidence of any transitional fossils, to show that evolution has occurred in the past, but there is absolutely no evidence of any evolutionary processes taken place today.

Why is there such a dogmatic adherence, by the scientific community to the evolution theory, in the lack of any evidence of such taking place? It is simple; to admit that evolution in the natural world does not exist, would mean that there had to be a creator.

Professor D.M.S. Watson, a leading evolutionary biologist of his day, demonstrates the anti-God thinking that motivates the evolutionist:

"Evolution is a theory universally accepted not because it can be proven by logically coherent evidence to be true, but because the only alternative, special creation, is clearly incredible." [110]

If creation is true, then there is a God, and if there is a God, then heaven and hell and the coming judgment are likewise real. Incarnate mankind with his inborn sinful nature does not want to hear that he will be judged for his sins. Satan and his demons are busy; they will mislead man any way possible, and that includes through evolution.

Science involves the observation and measurements of nature and the natural processes. When evolutionists go beyond what is observable and measurable it is no longer scientific; it is merely speculation. It is a theory, the theory of evolution. Therefore there is no demand that it be a proven fact, it is simply a theory. The problem lies in that it is being taught as if it is a proven fact. Science must be able to observe, measure, test and repeat the process before it can be considered a scientific fact, and this is simply not possible with the prehistoric past, as today's scientists weren't there.

---

109 Charles Darwin, *The Origin of Species,* Skyros Publishing, ,2015, p. 80 & 157
110 D.M.S. Watson, *Adaptation,* Nature, 124:233, 1929

When man attempts to rewrite the history of the universe and the origin and development of man and the earth, he is no longer in the field of science but has entered into the field of metaphysics. He is no longer working with demonstrated and established facts that can be proven, but with theory and hypotheses. There is no quarrel with modern geology in projecting theories to arrive at the truth. The problem arises when these hypotheses and theories are presented or applied as established facts.

An example of this indoctrination of students is revealed in a recent book, by the prestigious National Academy of Science. This publication entitled *Teaching about Evolution and Nature of Science,* has been made available to educators throughout America. It supposedly contains the latest information on evolution and is very professionally done. It is designed to encourage teachers to incorporate more evolution in their classes. It is extremely biased against God, and contains false information such as the following quote shows:

"However, in many cases, such as between primitive fish and amphibians, amphibians and reptiles, reptiles and mammals, and reptiles and birds, there are excellent transitional fossils."[111]

In the book, they provide no examples or evidence of the supposedly transitional fossils. Where is the proof for such a statement? Obviously, there is none, because none truly exists. This is nothing more than misinformation, designed to reinforce the evolution theory in the minds of the students. Sadly, this is not an isolated incident.

We will deal with the lack of transitional fossils in the following chapter, *The Fossil Record.*

Professor Alfred Rehwinkel, concerning the teaching of evolution as if it was a proven fact:

"As soon as a theory is presented as truth, is has become pseudoscience, mere quackery and is a hindrance to truth." [112]

It would seem however that when it comes to evolution, truth matters very little. For instance, if a theologian or even a scientist

---

111 Jonathan D. Sarfati, *Refuting Evolution,* Green Forest, Ar.,*Master Books, 2002,* p53
112 Alfred M. Rehwinkel, *The Flood*: *In the Light of the Bible, Geology, and Archaeology,* St. Louis, Mo., Concordia Publishing House, 1951

makes a statement based on the Bible, he is ridiculed as naive and clinging to outmoded beliefs and myths. But on the other hand, if an evolutionist makes a wild claim based on unverified assumptions, it is soon considered a fact and repeated as such.

Darwin, greatly influenced by Lydell, extended the principle of uniformity to biology. Darwin held that the forces we see today in the biologic world (reproduction, inheritance, and competition), through natural selection gradually produced the entire diversity of life on Earth.

There are two paramount reasons why biological evolution should be considered invalid. First is that there has never been observed, a process where life has come from non-life. Scientists have tried, but have never been successful. Despite what people think, life has never been created in a test tube. Life has never been observed to come from non-life. Therefore, to claim it has is unscientific. The scientific Law of Biogenesis states that observations have shown that life only comes from life. Second, there is no known process by which genetic information can be added to an organism's genetic code. If an organism's DNA cannot be added to, then it is impossible for any organism to evolve into a higher form. Science has demonstrated that over time living organisms lose genetic information; they do not gain it. Biological evolution is simply not possible. The Bible makes it clear that all creatures were created accordingly to their own kind. (Genesis 1:24)

The shortcomings of the theory of evolution were pointed out quite effectively in Dr. Jerry Fodor's article titled *"Why Pigs Don't Have Wings."* [113] And also in a book, co-authored by Dr. Massimo Piattelli-Palmarini, titled *"What Darwin Got Wrong."* [114]

Fodor presented a very serious challenge to the theory of evolution and natural selection. As a result, in July 2008, sixteen of the world's leading evolutionary scientists met in a castle in Altenberg, Austria, to discuss these serious threats to evolutionary science. They realize that if the evolutionary process of natural selection is rejected than Darwin's theory is dead.[115]

---

113 Jerry Fodor, *Why Pigs Don't Have Wings,* London Review of books, vol. 29, no. 20, 2007, p.19-22
114 Jerry Fodor and Massimo Piattelli-Palmarini, *What Darwin Got Wrong,* New York, Farrar, Straus, and Giroux, 2010
115 John Ashton, *Evolution Impossible,* Master Books, Green Forest, Ar., 2012

We are too unique to have randomly evolved. The Bible tells us that we are *"fearfully and wonderfully made."* (Ps 139:14) The following examples are just a few of the things that show how unique our bodies are, and how ridiculous the idea that we randomly evolved is.

Our bodies contain one hundred trillion cells. Each cell contains enough genetic information to fill 4,000 books five hundred pages in length. If every cell in one's person body were reduced to its 4,000 books, it would fill the Grand Canyon seventy-eight times.[116]

"The moon is 240,000 miles from Earth. If the DNA in a human cell were stretched out and connected, it would be over seven feet in length. If all this DNA in one person's body were placed end to end, it would extend to the moon 552,000 times." [117]

"The human brain contains ten thousand million nerve cells and contains over a hundred thousand million electrical connections… ….a much greater number of specific connections than in the entire communication network on earth." [118]

"The eye is such a marvelous thing. There are 10 million or more cells interacting with each other in such complex ways, it would take a minimum of 100 years of a Cray supercomputer to simulate what takes place in your eye many times every second." [119]

Life is simply too complex to have evolved at random.

"The complexity of the simplest known type of cell is so great that it is impossible to accept that such an object could have been thrown together suddenly by some kind freakish, vastly improbable, event. Such an occurrence would be indistinguishable from a miracle." [120]

The complexity of life is not just limited to humans; there are many examples in nature. Even the extinct and supposedly very

---

116 Carl Sagan, *The Dragons of Eden*, New York, Random House, 1977
117 Ibid
118 Michael Denton, *Evolution: A Theory in Crisis*, London, Burnett Books, 1985, p 330-331
119 David Menton, *Can Evolution Produce an Eye? Not a Chance!*, Missouri Assoc. for Creation, Inc., 1994
120 Michael Denton, *Evolution: A Theory in Crisis*, London, Burnett Books, 1985, p 330-331

primitive trilobites had quite complex eyes comprised of tubes pointing in different directions and special lenses that focused light from any distance. Trilobites would require an enormous amount of new genetic code to program their cells to produce the complex structure of this organism, yet despite the abundance of trilobite fossils, there is no fossil evidence of their evolution.[121]

The missing link is missing

In the millions of fossils that exist, there is an abundance of the young and old of many different species. In fact, we can trace many species from the embryonic stage to the adult stage. Why then is there no fossils links which would bind species together? Where is the missing link? Obviously, it is missing, there simply are none, as the following statements verify.

"One hundred and fifty years have already passed during which it has been said that the evolution of the species is a fact but, without giving real proofs of it and without even a principle of explaining it. During the last one hundred and fifty years of research that has been carried out along this line (in order to prove the theory), there has been no discovery of anything. It is simply a repetition in different ways of what Darwin said in 1859. This lack of results is unforgivable in a day when molecular biology has really opened the veil covering the mystery of reproduction and heredity." [122]

"Each class at a molecular level is unique, isolated and unlinked by intermediates. Thus molecules, like fossils, have failed to provide the elusive intermediates so long sought by evolutionary biology." [123]

"In terms of their biochemistry, none of the species deemed 'intermediate', 'ancestral' or 'primitive' by generations of evolutionary biologists, and alluded to as evidence of sequence in nature, show any sign of their supposed intermediate status." [124]

---

121 John F. Ashton, *Evolution Impossible: 12 Reasons Why Evolution Cannot Explain the Origin of Life on Earth,* Green Forest, Ar., Master Books, 2012
122 G. Salet, *Hasard et Certitude: Le Transformisme dent la Biologie Actuelle, 1973,* p. 331.
123 Michael Denton, *Evolution: A Theory in Crisis,* London, Burnett Books, 1985, p 330-331
124 Ibid

"All species appear fully developed, not partially developed. They show design. There are no examples of half-developed feathers, eyes, skin, tubes (arteries, veins, intestines, etc.), or any of thousands of other vital organs. Tubes that are not 100% complete are a liability; so are partially developed organs and some body parts. For example, if a leg of a reptile were to evolve into a wing of a bird, it would become a bad leg long before it became a good wing." [125]

Even evolutionists are well aware of the lack of evidence of intermediate species, as two evolutionary rodent authorities admit when their attempt to trace the rodent family tree failed.

"Indeed, from a quick look at the fossil record, it is easy to get the impression that rodents have always been rodents" [126]

Microevolution

Changes within a species, such as the different breeds of dogs and cows, for instance, are not evolution. These changes in size, shape, color, or minor genetic changes are referred to as microevolution. Microevolution falls under Mendel's laws of genetics. Mendel discovered that genes are merely reshuffled from one generation to another. Different combinations are formed, not different genes. The different combinations produce many variations within each kind of life, such as in the dog family. Adaptation is God's way of letting animals survive in different environments and climates. An Alaskan Huskie that has adapted to the cold and snow with its long hair and larger size is far different than a chihuahua that has adapted to a hot climate with its smaller size, short hair, and large ears. They are both, however, still dogs and contain the same genes that the original dog/wolf contained. They are simply arranged in different combinations. There are fixed limits to the variations possible. Any changes to an organism must remain within its distinct boundaries. Adaptation or changes due to specific breeding are not evolution. Genes are not randomly changed within an organism. A dog will always be a dog, and a cow will always be a cow.

---

125 Walt Brown, *In the Beginning: Compelling Evidence for Creation and the Flood*, Center for Scientific Creation, Phoenix, Az. 2001
126 Lionel Hautier and Philip G. Cox, Rodentia: a model order?, Evolution of the Rodents, Cambridge University Press, 2015, p.4

As more scientific discoveries are made, the theory of evolution becomes harder and harder to defend. Dr. John Ashton speaks of this in his excellent book *"Evolution Impossible."*

"I could find not a single published scientific paper reporting the evidence that supports the fundamental requirement of evolution that new meaningful genetic information arises by chance. Instead, I have found much published data showing that it is impossible for new purposeful genetic information of any significance for evolution to arise by chance." [127]

"Finally, there is only one attitude which is possible as I have just shown: It consists in affirming that: Intelligence comes before life. Many people will say, this is not science, it is philosophy. The only thing I am interested in is fact, and this conclusion comes out of an analysis and observation of the facts." [128]

Christian Schwabe alludes to the problem with evolutionists of refusing to acknowledge the problems that evolution faces as new facts come to light;

"One might ask why the neo-darwinian paradigm does not weaken or disappear if it is at odds with critical factual information. The reasons are not necessarily scientific ones but rather may be rooted in human nature." [129]

It should be noted that not all scientists agree with the theories of uniformitarianism and evolution. There are thousands of scientists that disagree with the theory of evolution. The Creation Research Society has over seven hundred scientists on its rolls alone. While many scientists disagree completely, many others are of the opinion that nothing has been proven either way. There are some scientists that accept evolution simply because of the myth that all scientists believe in evolution. Those that don't accept evolution as a proven fact tend to keep their opinions to themselves, rather

---

[127] John Ashton, *Evolution Impossible,* Master Books, Green Forest, Ar., 2012, p.22
[128] G. Salet, *Hasard et Certitude: Le Transformisme dent la Biologie Actuelle,* 1973, p. 331.
[129] Christian Schwabe, *On the Validity of Molecular Evolution, Trends in Biochemical Sciences,* July 1986, p. 282

than be criticized, discredited or as in some instances lose their positions. Israeli Education Ministry chief scientist Dr. Gavriel Avital was recently fired for questioning the validity of evolution.[130]

Even though evolution is taught in our schools and universities as if it is a proven fact, rather than simply a theory, it is still amazing how many people still believe in creation. A recent Gallup poll found that nearly half of Americans believe that God created humans in their present form 10,000 years ago, a view that has changed little over the past three decades. Half of Americans believe humans evolved, with the majority of these saying God guided the evolutionary process.[131]

The very philosophy of evolution denies the act of creation and the very existence of God. It denies that man was created in the image of God. Since man has evolved higher than the animals, he is the master of the planet. Evolution teaches that creation is taking place through nature's evolutionary processes, even though this contradicts the basic laws of science. Evolution takes the focus from God and places it on man. It is the basis for all the anti-God systems that have plagued mankind. It was the basis for Hitler's Nazism and Karl Marx's supposed scientific basis for communism.

Sir Julian Huxley, a prominent British evolutionary biologist, stated the evolutionist's view and belief quite plainly:

"In the evolutionary pattern of thought there is no longer either need or room for the supernatural. The earth was not created; it evolved. So did all the animals and plants that inhabit it, including our human selves, mind and soul, as well as brain and body. So did religion." [132]

Evolution is not science as evolutionists would have you believe. It is an anti-God system that's underlying purpose is to remove God from our lives and make man his own God. That fact is confirmed by evolutionary biologist Richard Dickerson:

"Science is fundamentally a game. It is a game with one overriding rule: Rule #1: Let us see how far and to what extent we can explain

---

130 Haaretz, *Sa'ar Dismisses Chief Scientist For Questioning Evolution*, Oct. 5, 2010, www.haaretz.com
131 Gallup Poll, *Americans' views related to religiousness, age, education*
132 Julian Huxley, Essays of a Humanist, Harper & Row, New York, 1964, pp.82-83

the behavior of the physical and material universe in terms of purely physical and material causes, without invoking the supernatural." [133] Evolution is the religion of atheism, a religion that will not allow them to even consider that there is an omnipotent creator God. "Even if all the data point to an intelligent designer, such a hypothesis is excluded from science because it is not naturalistic." [134]

"we are forced by our *a priori* adherence to material causes to create an apparatus of investigation and a set of concepts that produce material explanations, no matter how counter-intuitive, no matter how mystifying to the uninitiated. Moreover, that materialism is absolute, for we cannot allow a Divine Foot in the door." [135]

Jesus said "Make a tree good and its fruit will be good, or make a tree bad and its fruit will be bad, for a tree is recognized by its fruit (Matthew 12:33). The fruit of evolution is an evil fruit. Its effects on man have been harmful and degrading. It has tried to destroy the relationship between God and man. Indeed, millions have been denied that relationship through such anti-God systems as Nazism and Communism. The philosophy of evolution and uniformitarianism has eroded and is still eroding the belief in the creator God.

How many hundreds of thousands of students have been turned away from God by the atheistic teaching of evolution by mislead professors? Such as evolutionary entomologist and sociobiologist E.O.Wilson admits to:

"As were many persons from Alabama, I was a born-again Christian. When I was fifteen, I entered the Southern Baptist Church with great fervor and interest in the fundamentalist religion; I left at seventeen when I got to the University of Alabama and heard about evolutionary theory." [136]

George Campbell Morgan, evangelist, and leading Bible scholar grew up in a Christian home, never questioning that the Bible was the Word of God. But in college, he encountered skeptics who shook

---

133 R.E.Dickerson, *Molecular Evolution,* 34:277, 1992, Perspective on Science and the Christian Faith, 44:137-138,1992
134 Scott C.Todd, *A View from Kansas on the Evolution Debates,* Nature, Vol. 401, September 30, 1999, p. 423.
135 Richard Lewontin, Review of the Demon-Haunted World, by Carl Sagan. In New York Review of Books, January 9, 1997.
136 E.O. Wilson, *The Humanist,* September/ October, 1982, p40

his faith. "The whole intellectual world was under the mastery of the physical scientists," he recalled. "There came a moment when I was sure of nothing." Fortunately, he turned to the Bible for answers.

How powerful the influence professors have over their students is demonstrated by this comment from physicist Mark Singham, speaking on the trust that college students have for their professors and in what they are being taught.

"And I use that trust to effectively brainwash them.......We only introduce arguments and evidence that supports the currently accepted theories and omit or gloss over any evidence to the contrary." [137]

Is evolution one of Satan's weapons in his age-long rebellion against his Creator? As Christians, we must continually be on guard against Satan's ploys to lead people away from God. Satan has found that rather than an obvious frontal attack against our salvation, it is much more efficient to misdirect or mislead people through false religions, beliefs and yes, even evolution. Evolution masquerading as science makes an effective tool for Satan.

"One can have a religious view that is compatible with evolution only if the religious view is indistinguishable from atheism." [138]

"Evolution is, indeed, the pseudo-scientific basis of religious atheism." [139]

I know this may not be a very popular view, but as Christians, we must test all things according to the Scriptures. We have the ultimate reference and history book in the Bible. God has made known to us everything from the very first day of creation on. We have an account of creation, the flood, the birth of Christ, the way of salvation and the coming end time events. We know the Bible is the divine word of God. The enormous amount of evidence proving it is simply overwhelming.

---

137 Singham, Mark, "Teaching and Propaganda," Physics Today (vol. 53, June 2000), p. 54.
138 Will Provine, "No Free Will," in Catching Up with the Vision, ed. by Margaret W. Rossiter, Chicago: University of Chicago Press, 1999, p. S123.
139 Henry M. Morris, The Scientific Case Against Evolution, Institute For Creation Research, http://www.icr.org/home/resources/resources_tracts_scientificcaseagainstevolution/

There is nothing in the Bible that has been proven to be incorrect. There are over 2000 prophecies that have been fulfilled, many down to very specific details, that prove the scriptures to be accurate and God inspired. Archaeology has continued to demonstrate the accuracy of the Bible. Not once, has an archaeology find disagreed with the Word of God. With this in mind, as a Christian when conflict arises between science and the Bible, we must always choose the divine word of the omnipotent God over man's limited knowledge that he calls science.

CHAPTER 17

The Fossil Record

MOST OF THE LAND surface of the earth is covered or underlain with sedimentary rock. Sedimentary rock is made up of sand, gravel, clay and silt which were eroded and transported by water, and finally deposited by moving water. As the name implies, sedimentary rocks are made up of sediment.

Such sedimentary rocks are what contain the fossils. There has never been a time or event more ideal than the Great Flood for burying enormous numbers of fossils. Fossils are the remains of living things, and for fossils to form it is necessary for the organism to be buried quickly, the circumstances have to be just right for fossilization to occur. Bones or shells of animals, reptiles, or fishes may occasionally be trapped in some sediment and be buried, but this is not a normal or frequent occurrence. The few fossils forming today can only happen after being rapidly buried by water.

The billions of fossils that are found in huge fossil graveyards around the world could have only come from a catastrophic event such the Flood. In the present era, there is never found large deposits of organisms buried together and waiting for fossilization, yet this is exactly what has happened in the past.

For example, fossil deposits near Fossil, Wyoming included mammals, birds, crustaceans, Molluscs, reptiles, fish, plants and a large variety of insects. Among these were an alligator, bats, palm trees, palmetto frond, sunfish, sea bass, two different extinct stingrays, turtles, snipe, pickerel, a chicken-like bird, an extinct tapir and crocodile, a horse-like mammal, a nearly six-foot soft shelled turtle plus several extinct animals and fishes.[140]

The gold-bearing gravel of the Klondike and Nome was laid down under mild conditions, as is evident from the fossils that are found there. In this gold-bearing gravel, sometimes over a hundred feet below the surface, are the bones of mammals, such as bison, mammoth, elk, moose, buffalo, caribou, horse, and muskox. In this gravel and muck, the American Museum of Natural History reported finding mammoth remains with parts of the flesh covered with long black hair still intact and together with them the skull of a lion similar to the lion now found in Africa.[141]

In Cumberland Bone Cave in Maryland, forty-one genera of mammals were found, about sixteen percent of which are extinct. These included wolverine, grizzly bear, peccaries, an eland like antelope, groundhogs, saber tooth cats, mastodon, cave bear, musk ox, tapir, beaver and muskrat among others.[142]

This mixture of plants and animals from different regions and even different climates give credibility to the theory that the global climate was tropical and that all kinds of animals were distributed throughout the earth rather than being confined to certain regions. This mixing of organisms, all in one place, is typical of the most significant fossil deposits. There are hundreds of fossils beds worldwide, with many of these containing millions and even billions of fossils.

Here is a small sample of these beds: A fossil graveyard in Germany contains more than six thousand fossils of vertebrate animals and a great number insects, Mollusca and plants. It is estimated that there are more than eight hundred thousand million skeletons of vertebrate animals in the Karroo formation in South Africa. In the Miocene shale beds of California, there are more than a billion fish fossils on four square miles of bay bottom. A limestone fossil bed in Nebraska contains thousands of bones of rhinoceros, camels, giant boar, small gazelle, camels,

---

140 Wikipedia, *Fossil Butte National Monument,* http://en.wikipedia.org/wiki/Fossil_Butte_National_Monument, 2011

141 American Museum of Natural History, cited in Rehwinkel, Alfred M., *The Flood,* St. Louis, Mo., Concordia Publishing House, 1951

142 *Maryland Department of Natural Resources,* http://dnr.maryland.gov/naturalresource/fall2006/cave.

bear, dogs and numerous more exotic and extinct animals. These were all found all jumbled together in the stratum.[143]

To try and account for these vast fossil deposits by the typical slow present day processes is entirely impossible. Only a catastrophic event could entomb such enormous numbers and variety of creatures and plants. And only massive flood waters could carry and deposit such large numbers and variety of creatures into an area. Considering the magnitude and nature of the Genesis Flood, it would appear to be the perfect explanation for the vast fossil beds worldwide.

In today's natural processes it is rare for an organism to become fossilized. When most living organisms die, they are usually scavenged by other living creatures or they simply decay.

"When a fish dies its body floats on the surface or sinks to the bottom and is devoured rather quickly, actually in a matter of hours, by other fish. However, the fossil fish found in sedimentary rocks is very often preserved with all its bones intact. Entire shoals of fish over large areas, numbering billions of specimens, are found in a state of agony, but with no mark of a scavenger's attack." [144]

"It is significant that fossils, especially of large animals such as the dinosaurs, must be buried quickly or they will not be preserved at all. Furthermore, the sediments entrapping them must harden into stone fairly quickly, inhibiting the action of air, bacteria, etc., or else they will soon be decomposed and disappear. The very nature of fossilization thus seems to require catastrophism. Most certainly must this be true of the great dinosaur beds, the massive fish-bearing shales, the tremendous deposits of elephants and other animals in the arctic regions, and the great numbers of other "fossil graveyards" with which the geologic column abound." [145]

There were no fossils before the fall of mankind because there was no death before then. In fact, there were probably very few fossils from before the great Flood. When Adam sinned, the earth fell under the curse as well as man. (Genesis 3:17)

---

143 John C. Whitcomb and Henry M. Morris, *The Genesis Flood,* Phillipsburg, N.J., Presbyterian And Reformed Publishing Co., 1989
144 Immanuel Velikovsky, *Earth in Upheaval,* New York, Doubleday and Co., 1955.
145 Henry M. Morris and Martin E. Clark, *The Bible Has The Answer,* Green Forest, AR., Master Books, 2005

"Therefore, just as sin entered the world through one man, and death through sin, and in this way death came to all people, because all sinned" (Romans 7:12)

According to the Scriptures, death was non-existent before the fall. This would include everything from the simplest life forms to man himself. Any fossils found would have come from animals that died after man's fall. The fossil record contained in the sedimentary rocks is a record of sudden death on a global scale. Sedimentary rocks are the only rocks that contain fossils. For fossils to have been preserved, the sediment that made up these rocks would have had to been laid down quickly under flood conditions. In the entire history of the world, there has never been a more ideal condition for the creation of large numbers of fossils, then during the great deluge. Conditions have to be almost perfect for fossils to form. Today we see relatively few fossils being formed. Only the global flood can account for such large numbers of fossils contained within the sedimentary rocks

"Comparatively few remains of organisms now inhabiting the earth are being deposited under conditions favorable for their preservation as fossils." [146]

"Present-day processes are forming very few potential fossil deposits....Nothing comparable to the tremendous fossiliferous beds of fish, mammals, reptiles, etc that are found in many places around the world is being formed today.....uniformity and modern processes cannot legitimately account for the fossil deposits." [147]

The global flood is the perfect explanation as to how the fossils were buried. The worms, slugs, etc. would have been buried first. Followed by the heavier and simpler life forms, such as shellfish that were near the bottom and would have been trapped and buried earlier and deeper in the sediment deposited by the flood waters. Marine vertebrates such as fish would have been higher in the sediment, with amphibians and reptiles above them. More complex creatures that were more mobile would have become entrapped later and buried higher up in the sediment. The more

---

146 William J. Miller, *An Introduction to Historical Geology*, New York, Van Nostrand, 1952
147 John C. Whitcomb and Henry M. Morris, *The Genesis Flood*, Phillipsburg, N.J., Presbyterian And Reformed Publishing Co., 1989

active creatures that had the ability to run, swim or fly, would have buried even higher. Because of the violent nature of the flood, there would be exceptions to this order of course, but as a general rule, this is the way the fossil record occurs, and the flood is the perfect explanation for it.

The evolutionist, however, sees this sequence of how fossils are buried as being proof that it was how life evolved. The fossil record in the sedimentary rocks is supposed to show the evolution of life into more advanced and complex life forms, over vast spans of time. The fossil record is by far the most important evidence for the theory of evolution. The ironic part of this is, without the fossil record from the flood, the evolutionist would have no basis for their theories.

"Fossils provide the only historical, documentary evidence that life has evolved from simpler to more and more complex forms." [148]

"Instead of being acknowledged as evidence of the great Flood, however, these fossil deposits have instead been interpreted as demonstrating organic evolution! In fact, it is widely recognized by evolutionists that the fossil sequences supply the only apparent historical evidence that evolution has really occurred on more than a trivial scale. All other suggested evidence for evolution--mutations, geographic distribution, anatomical resemblances, etc.--are strictly circumstantial in nature and can easily be explained in terms of special creation and the general Biblical framework of interpretation." [149]

Man has taken the fossil record, which should have been proof of the flood, and turned it around to fit his own reasoning.

"In the days of Noah, men, animals, and trees,.....were buried, and thus preserved as an evidence to later generations that the antediluvians perished by a flood. God designed that the discovery of these things should establish faith in inspired history; but men, with their vain reasoning, fall into the same error as did the people before the Flood--the thing which God gave them as a benefit, they turn into a curse by making a wrong use of them." [150]

---

148 Dunbar, C.O., *Historical Geology, Second Edition*, John Wiley, New York, 1960, p. 47.
149 Henry M. Morris, *Studies In The Bible And Science*, Philadelphia, PA., Presbyterian and Reformed Publishing Co., 1966.
150 Ibid

Fossils are so abundant in sedimentary rocks that they are almost universally used as the main means of identifying the geologic age of a particular rock. Many times supposedly more ancient fossils are found on top of more recent fossils. When this happens, it is assumed that it is because of movement of the earth by up thrusts, folds or over thrusts that changed the positions of the fossils. This is commonly believed even when there is no indication of such movements having taken place.

Again, it is not the data or evidence of the flood that we have a disagreement with the evolutionists about, but rather the interpretation of that data. God has left evidence of the flood and its effects, all of which can be interpreted within the guideline of the Bible quite easily. The fossil record does not show the order that life evolved, but merely the order that they were buried in the great flood.

There are few cases of human skeletal remains being found in ancient strata. It is to be expected that few such specimens would be found. The intelligence and mobility of antediluvian men would have caused them to be moving to higher ground in the initial weeks of the Flood. The result would be fewer bodies buried and fossilized. Most would have been floating and decaying. Moreover, the explicit purpose of the Flood was to destroy that wicked civilization (Genesis 6:5-7). Nonetheless, there has been a few human fossil finds such as the Guadeloupe skeletons which were embedded in Miocene (16-23 million years ago), limestone strata. Numerous human remains have been found in coal deposits which are supposedly 300 million years old. In a Moab, Utah copper mine fossilized human skeletons were discovered in Cretaceous-age sandstone (supposedly more than 65 million years old).[151] All of these were millions of years before man supposedly evolved according to the evolution timescale. Rather than acknowledge this finds, evolutionists just tend to ignore them. For to accept them, would destroy the theory of evolution.

Tools, implements, and artifacts have been found embedded deep in coal mines, stone quarries and other strata. There have been items such as a large ceramic spoon or ladle that was found in the ashes of a coal stove by a woman in Pennsylvania in 1937. Other items include cut iron nails, gold thread, a tapered iron screw, bronze coin, doll, cast

---

151 Genesis Park, *Ancient Human Skeletons,* http://www.genesispark.com, 2015

iron pot, an intricate gold chain, a puzzling iron cube, and strange-looking iron thimble, just to name a few.

A bell-shaped vessel of exquisite workmanship was discovered fifteen feet underground, at Dorchester, Mass. The sides are inlaid with images of flowers, fines or a wreath. The object appeared to be a composition of metals and inlaid with silver.

A brass ornate bell was discovered in a lump of West Virginia coal. The Institute for Creation Research had the bell submitted to the lab at the University of Oklahoma. There a nuclear activation analysis revealed that the bell contains an unusual mix of metals, different from any known modern alloy production (including copper, zinc, tin, arsenic, iodine, and selenium).[152] Genesis 4:22 states that Tubal-Cain was "an instructor of every artificer in brass and iron..."

---

152 *Amazing Bible Discoveries, www.6000years.org, 2015*

In June 1936, Max Hahn and his wife Emma were on a walk when they noticed a rock with wood protruding from its core. They decided to take the oddity home and later cracked it open with a hammer and a chisel. Ironically, what they found within seemed to be an archaic hammer of sorts. A team of archaeologists checked it, and as it turns out, the rock encasing the hammer was dated back more than 400 million years; the hammer itself turned out to be more than 500 million years old. Additionally, a section of the handle has begun the transformation to coal. [153] These objects were supposedly buried in coal and rocks that were millions of years old, which according to evolution, would have been millions of years before man walked on the earth. A more likely scenario would be that they are antediluvian objects and were buried during the great flood in a mass of vegetation, which over time became coal or rock. The scientific establishment will never admit to these artifacts as being authentic. To do so would be to admit that the whole theory of evolution is wrong. Anything that doesn't fit into their thinking is simply ignored or they attempt to explain it away, as evolutionist Stephen Gould stated:

"Facts do not speak for themselves; they are read in light of theory" [154]

In other words, the facts are made to fit the theory, rather than the theory being made to represent the actual facts. This attitude results in far different interpretations of the same scientific data than that of the creationist. Evolutionist Boyce Rensberger writes:

"The fact is that scientists are not really as objective and dispassionate in their work as they would like you to think. Most scientists first get their ideas about how the world works not through rigorously logical processes but through hunches and wild guesses. As individuals, they often come to believe something to be true long before they assemble the hard evidence that will convince somebody else that it is." [155]

"There can be no observations without an immense apparatus of preexisting theory. Before sense experiences become "observations" we need a theoretical question, and what counts as a relevant

---

153 Ibid
154 Stephen Jay Gould, *Ever Since Darwin*, W.W. Norton, New York, 1977, p161-162
155 Boyce Rensberger, *How the World Works*, NY, William Morrow, 1986, p18

observation depends upon a theoretical frame into which it is to be placed. Repeatable observations that do not fit into an existing frame have a way of disappearing from view, and the experiments that produced them are not revisited." [156]

With a mindset like that, it is hard to imagine anything ever changing, even though the evidence against evolution continues to mount up. In fact, there is so much evidence now available that if the theory of evolution were presented today if would probably be outright rejected immediately. Sadly evolution has been ingrained into the scientific community so thoroughly that it will probably never change until the Lord returns.

Living Fossils: "Living fossils" are plants or animals that closely resemble species known from fossils but have no close living relatives by evolutionary reckoning. However, there are numerous species of plants and animals that the evolutionists had declared extinct, millions of years ago but have turned up alive and well, living in the modern world. A world that they supposedly were not equipped to live in and hence evolution had passed them by for more advanced species.

The Tuatara, the sole survivor of the reptilian order of beakheads, was supposed to have become extinct 135 million years ago, but we now know it lives in New Zealand.

In the winter of 1938, a fishing boat off the coast of southern Africa dragged from the Indian Ocean, a fish that supposedly lived 350

---

156 Richard Lewontin, Review of the Demon-Haunted World, by Carl Sagan. In New York Review of Books, January 9, 1997.

million years ago and was thought to be extinct for 70 million years. The Coelacanth are from the Crossopterygii, a group that is supposed to be ancestral to land vertebrates. It was considered an index fossil. Any rock which contained a Coelacanth fossil was believed to be 70,000,000 to 400,000,000 years old. No fossils of coelacanths have ever been found in the same layers as human fossils, but they have been found in the same layers as dinosaur fossils. Paleontologists had confidently pronounced the coelacanth was extinct before man had evolved. Nevertheless, humans and coelacanths are living together in the present world. Another one was caught, thousands of miles away in Indonesia in 1998.[157] Several more have been caught since.

The discovery of the Coelacanth was an embarrassment to the evolutionist, in that the Coelacanth was considered to be the chief candidate to represent a transition species from fish to amphibian. Supposedly one hundred million years ago, the Coelacanth walked out the water on its fins, grew legs and became an amphibian. However, they are still the same as they were supposedly a hundred million years ago. The evolutionist believed the Coelacanth lived in shallow water, ready to crawl out onto land, when in fact, it was a deep sea fish. Its discovery was a blow to the evolution theory as the following statements show.

"Before live coelacanths were caught, evolutionists incorrectly believed the coelacanth had lungs, a large brain, and four bottom fins *about to evolve into legs*. Evolutionists reasoned that the coelacanth, or a similar fish, must have crawled out of a shallow sea, filled its lungs with air, becoming the first four-legged, land animal. Millions of students have been taught that this fish was the ancestor of all amphibians, reptiles, dinosaurs, birds and mammals, including people." [158]

"Throughout the hundreds of millions of years the coelacanths have kept the same form and structure. Here is one of the great mysteries of evolution." [159]

"The brain of a 90-pound coelacanth weighs less than 50 grams

---

157 BBC News, *Fisherman catches 'Living Fossil'*, August 1, 2007, http://news.bbc.co.uk
158 Walt Brown, *In The Beginning: Compelling Evidence for Creation and the Flood*, Center for Scientific Creation, Phoenix, Az. 2001
159 Jacques Millot, *The Coelacanth, Scientific American*, Vol. 193, Dec. 1955, p. 37

[0.11 ounces]—that is, no more than one 15,000th of the body weight. No present-day vertebrate that we know of has so small a brain in relation to its size." [160]

".....We never saw any of them walk, and it appears the fish is unable to do so." [161]

The coelacanth, the fish that the evolutionists claimed walked out of the water and became one of the first amphibians, is alive and well today. But it is still a fish, just as God made it.

The modern Huntsman spider is a very active spider native to the tropics and southern Europe. A recent Huntsman spider was found preserved in Baltic amber. Baltic amber is commonly dated by evolutionists at 35–50 million years old based on surrounding rocks. Thus, the Huntsman spider being examined is believed by the researchers to be 50 million years old. Evidently, Huntsman spiders didn't know they were supposed to evolve, for his modern descendants appear identical to him.[162]

On May 6, 1952, ten living specimens of an extraordinary mollusk were discovered while trawling off the Pacific coast of Costa Rica; the Danish deep-sea "Galathea" expedition hauled these specimens from a depth of 11,700 feet in the Acapulco Trench. They were given the name *Neopilina Galathea*. The newfound mollusks are living representative of Monoplacophora, a class of mollusk that was supposed to have become extinct about 280 million years ago.[163]

The conifer genus Metasequoia was considered to have become extinct some 20 million years ago was discovered growing in a remote region of China.

A collection of Wollemi Pines were discovered in the Blue

---

160 Ibid
161 Hans Fricke, "Coelacanths: The Fish That Time Forgot", *National Geographic*, Vol. 173, June 1988, p. 837.
162 Elizabeth Mitchell, *Tropical Huntsman, Answers in Genesis, May 2011*
163 John C. Whitcomb and Henry M. Morris, The Genesis Flood, Phillipsburg, N.J., Presbyterian And Reformed Publishing Co., 1989

Mountains, west of Sydney, Australia, when park ranger David Noble stumbled across the unusual trees. The species had been thought to have been extinct for at least two million years.[164]

In the April 2007 issue of the science journal *Nature* describes two recent discoveries of the world's oldest (allegedly) tree fossils. The study's lead author, paleobotanist William Stein of New York's Binghamton University, describes the fossilized tree as looking like "a palm tree, or perhaps a tree fern." According to Stein, the trees "belong to a previously known plant group called cladoxylopsids." Apparently, these oldest of trees, supposedly at least 385 million years old, waved in the breeze just like a modern palm tree.[165]

Here's the two-part "problem" (for evolutionists) with living fossils: first, living fossils show that advanced features had far less time to evolve than what evolutionists suspected; evolving from primordial goo to complex life in a billion years would be "hard enough" without such living fossils reducing the timeframe. Second, living fossils present the problem of apparently having had no modification despite supposed millions of years of natural selection.

In other words, there are many trees similar in form and feature to these newfound fossil trees, but their differences are substantial enough that Stein (and other evolutionists) can't connect them in an evolutionary lineage.[166]

A sponge called Nucha was found in the upper Triassic of Vancouver Island, which was nearly identical to a Nucha fossil previously found only in the Middle Cambrian of New South Wales, Australia. According to the strata, they were found in, there would have been 300 million years between them. It would appear that evolutions time of 300 million years between the Cambrian and the Permian is not very realistic.

There are literally thousands of different types of animals and plants which are alive and essentially unchanged from the way they

---

164   BBC NEWS Science-Nature 9/25/2003 http://news.bbc.co.uk
165   John Roach, National Geographic News, April 18, 2007
166   Answers in Genesis, News to Note, April 21, 2007, A Tree for Today?

appear as fossils. Evolutionists claim that fossils are much older than they are, simply because they refuse to acknowledge the occurrence of the Biblical global flood and the effects upon the geology features of the earth. The Bible records that all plants and animals were created at the same time, the week of creation. The fact that many plants and animals are alive today having changed very little if any from their relatives that supposedly lived millions of years ago, should make the scientific community question their dating methods. The total lack of any visible evolutionary advancement in so many species of plants and animals should be a red flag that maybe there is no evolution of the species taking place. Add to that, the fact that man has been witness to millions of species of plants and animals having become extinct. But during the same time, there has been no evolution of any new plant or animal. It seems that the theory of evolution must take more faith to believe in, than believing that an omnipotent God created the plants and animals. Many evolutionists admit that the fossil record is completely lacking in any evidence of evolution whatsoever.

An example is Harvard evolutionist, Stephen Jay Gould: "I regard the failure to find a clear 'vector of progress' in life's history as the most puzzling fact of the fossil record." [167]

Another example from paleontologist David Kitts: "The fossil record doesn't even provide any evidence in support of the Darwinian theory except in the weak sense that the fossil record is compatible with it, just as it is compatible with other evolutionary theories, and revolutionary theories, and special creationist theories and even ahistorical theories." [168]

"Evolution, at least in the sense that Darwin speaks of it, cannot be detected within the lifetime of a single observer." [169]

David M. Raup, head of geology at the University of Chicago, an iconoclastic and influential paleontologist, who was one of the

---

167 Stephen Jay Gould, *The Ediacaran Experiment,* Natural History No. 93, February 1984, p.14-23.
168 David B Kitts, *Search for the Holy Transformation,* quoted from Institute for Creation Research, *Scientific Creationism*
169 David B. Kitts, *Paleontology and Evolutionary Theory, Evolution,* Vol. 28; September 1974, p. 466.

leading figures of evolutionary biology, speaks about the lack of evidence in the fossil record to support the evolution theory.

"Well, we are now about 120 years after Darwin and the knowledge of the fossil record has been greatly expanded. We now have a quarter of a million fossil species, but the situation hasn't changed much. The record of evolution is still surprisingly jerky and, ironically, we have even fewer examples of evolutionary transitions than we had in Darwin's time. By this I mean that some of the classic cases of darwinian change in the fossil record, such as the evolution of the horse in North America, have had to be discarded or modified as a result of more detailed information-- what appeared to be a nice simple progression when relatively few data were available now appear to be much more complex and much less gradualistic. So Darwin's problem has not been alleviated in the last 120 years and we still have a record which does show change but one that can hardly be looked upon as the most reasonable consequence of natural selection." [170]

"In the years after Darwin, his advocates hoped to find predictable progressions. In general, these have not been found-- yet the optimism has died hard, and some pure fantasy has crept into textbooks." [171]

Evolutionists admit that there are no evidence that they can point to as a transition species.
"This regular absence of transitional forms is not confined to mammals, but is an almost universal phenomenon, as has long been noted by paleontologists." [172]
"Paleontologists have paid an exorbitant price for Darwin's argument. We fancy ourselves as the only true students of life's history, yet to preserve our favored account of evolution by natural selection we view our data as so bad that we almost never see the very process we profess to study." [173]

---

170 David. M. Raup, *Conflicts between Darwin and Paleontology*, Field Museum of Natural History Bulletin, Jan. 1979
171 David M. Raup, *Evolution and the Fossil Record*, Science, Vol 213, July 17, 1981
172 George Gaylord Simpson, *Tempo and Mode in Evolution*, New York, Columbia University Press, 1944, p.106
173 Stephen Jay Gould, *The Panda's Thumb*, W. W. Norton & Company (1992), pp. 181-2.

"But fossil species remain unchanged throughout most of their history and the record fails to contain a single example of a significant transition." [174]

"The fossil record does not convincingly document a single transition from one species to another." [175]

The late Dr. Colin Patterson, senior paleontologist of the British Museum of Natural History, wrote concerning the lack of transition species in his book "Evolution":
"About the lack of direct illustrations in my book. If I knew of any, fossil or living, I would certainly have included them......I will lay it on the line--there is not one such fossil for which one could make a watertight argument." [176]

Even though there is no evidence within the fossil records to support evolution, there are a great many people who believe there is. This is mostly due to evolution has been claimed as a scientific fact, and has been taught in our universities as if it was fact rather than theory. The trouble is that even though evolution has not and cannot be proven, it has been propagated as scientific fact, to the point that even Christians are led astray. Another quote by professor and paleontologist David M. Raup, show how bad this problem is.

"One of the ironies of the evolution-creation debate is that the creationists have accepted the mistaken notion that the fossil record shows a detailed and orderly progression and they have gone to great lengths to accommodate this 'fact' in their Flood geology." [177]

---

174 David S. Woodruff, *Evolution: The Paleobiological View*, Science, Vol. 208, 16 May 1980, p. 716.
175 Steven M. Stanley, *The New Evolutionary Timetable*, New York, Basic Books Inc, 1981, p.95
176 Colin Patterson as cited in Jonathan Sarfati, *Refuting Evolution*, Green Forest, Ar. Master Books, 1999
177 David M. Raup, *Evolution and the Fossil Record*, Science, Vol 213, July 17,1981

CHAPTER 18

Dating Methods

CURRENT DATING METHODS ARE based on assumptions rather than any proof that they are accurate. They assume that changes in nature have occurred at the same rate from the beginning of time. They assume that God created a world that was lacking in certain key elements. They assume that changes in the earth and universe didn't affect the elements or their chemical changes. Only if scientists would have begun their testing when the world first began, would they know whether the current dating methods are accurate or not, and of course that is not possible. Therefore they just assume these methods are accurate, even though there is considerable evidence to suggest otherwise.

There are many different methods of dating the geologic features of the earth. Different methods will almost always give different results, for instance, one method may give a date for an object as being thousands of years old, while another method may date the same object as being millions or even billions of years old. Scientists simply use the one that will give an age within the range they believe the item is from.

The method of radiometric or radioactive dating is a process for determining the age of an object by measuring the amount of a given radioactive material it contains. There are numerous methods of radioactive dating such as potassium-argon dating, rubidium-strontium dating, carbon 14 dating, uranium-lead dating, etc. These are all methods that are based on measurements of either short-lived radioactive elements or the amount of a long-lived radioactive element plus its decay product. Since each of these methods will give different ages, the biologist will choose the method that will most likely give the date within the time period he believes to object to be from.

An example of different methods giving different dates is a rock from the Grand Canyon that various dating methods were used on. The rock was dated 656 million years old using potassium-argon. It is dated at 1075 million years old using rubidium-strontium dating. It is 1330 million years old when the age is determined by lead-lead dating, and it is only 1400 years old using samarium-neodymium dating[178] other methods give even more conflicting results.

There are flaws in the various dating methods that evolutionary scientists totally ignore, for instance with carbon-14 (radiocarbon) decays rather quickly. It has a half-life of only 5,730 years. This means that there should not be any radiocarbon left in fossils after a few thousand years, yet radiocarbon has been detected in fossils supposedly up to hundreds of millions of years old and in all diamonds which are supposedly 1–3 billion years old.

"Even if every atom in the whole earth were carbon-14, they would decay so quickly that no carbon-14 would be left on earth after only 1 million years."[179]

During the year that the waters covered the earth, with the removal of the vapor canopy, there would have been nothing to block the radiation during that time period. Therefore the amount of radiation hitting the earth would have been much greater than normal. Likewise from the time of creation until the great deluge, the amount of radiation hitting the earth would have been minor compared to today. The vapor canopy or water that was contained above the earth,(Genesis 1:7) would have blocked out most of the cosmic rays and harmful radiation. Both of these time periods would have greatly changed the amount of radiation available to the natural processes.

The Flood would have buried large amounts of carbon in the form of living plants and animals, which form our present day fossil fuels. From the enormous amount of these fossil fuels, it confirms the fact that plant life before the flood was much greater than it is today,

---

178 Marcel Toussaint, *The painful agony of the Evolutionist Myth: Scientific Weaknesses of the Evolution Theory*, BookRix, Amazon Digital Services LLC, 2016
179 Andrew A Snelling, *Carbon-14 in Fossils, Coal and Diamonds*, Answers Magazine, October 2012

which means that the amount of carbon would have been much greater during that period. All of the different dating methods are based on the assumption the natural processes have never changed. Obviously, that is not true, which makes any measurements using today's standards unreliable. Especially for any date that was prior to the end of the global flood.

Carbon-14 has shown not to be accurate beyond 2000 to 3000 years. With some organisms, it cannot be considered accurate at all. For instance, it has been found that the shells of living mollusks may show radiocarbon ages of up to 2300 years.[180]

There are many examples of the various methods of dating that have given results that are known to be in error by millions or even billions of years. Below are just a few of these examples:

Tests were conducted on rocks formed from the lava flow of the Hualalai Volcano in Hawaii which erupted between 1800 and 1801. A variety of radioisotope dating methods were used with each test producing different ages for the same sample. The age estimates ranged from 140 million to 2.96 billion years, (in reality they were only about two hundred years old). The same was found for Salt Lake Crater on Oahu. One test result dated a rock at 400,000 years. Others produced results ranging from 2.6 million to 3.3 billion. Not only do radioisotope dating give ages that are incorrect, but they don't even agree with each other.[181]

Underwater samples from the Mt. Kilauea lava flow were taken from a depth 4,680 meters. The eruption occurred about 200 years ago. The test results, using the radioisotope method of potassium to argon, dated the rocks at 21, plus or minus 8, million years. Samples taken from a depth of 3,420 meters dated it at 12, plus or minus 2, million years. And those taken from a depth of 1,400 meters were dated at zero. All of the samples were from the same lava flow.

Another example of a dating method giving 'dates' that are wrong for rocks of a known historical age, is the Potassium–argon,

---

180 M.L. Keith and G.M. Anderson, *Radiocarbon Dating: Fictitious Results with Mollusk Shells*, Science, August 16, 1963, p.634

181 Marcel Toussaint, *The painful agony of the Evolutionist Myth: Scientific Weaknesses of the Evolution Theory*, BookRix, Amazon Digital Services LLC, 2016

a radiometric dating method that was used at five lava flows from Mt Ngauruhoe in New Zealand. Although one lava flow occurred in 1949, three in 1954, and one in 1975, the 'dates' ranged from less than 0.27 to 3.5 million. The error was explained, that excess argon was retained in the rock when it solidified.[182]

A more recent example of dating methods giving the wrong date for rocks of known age are from a dacite lava dome at Mount St. Helens volcano that was formed in 1986 during the eruption there was dated (using the Potassium-Argon [K-Ar] method) at 0.35 ±0.05 million years.[183]

The secular scientific literature lists many examples of excess argon causing dates of millions of years in rocks of known historical age. This excess appears to have come from the upper mantle, below Earth's crust. This is consistent with a young world—the argon has had too little time to escape. If excess argon can cause exaggerated dates for rocks of known age, then why should we trust the method for rocks of unknown age?[184]

If radioactive dates of known rocks are given such ridiculously old ages in error, why are they still accepted for rocks of unknown ages?

Many geologists now believe that certain portions of the Grand Canyon, once thought to be up to 5 million years old (Marble Canyon and the Inner Gorge), may be as young as 600,000 years old.

Recent testing using various current testing methods have given ages from 100,000 years to 70 million years. That's quite a range, how can anyone have any confidence in any of the current dating techniques, with results like that?

"A real confidence builder in the reliability of geochronologists to actually know what they are talking about better than flipping a coin. I mean, pick your poison. It seems like, depending upon the method chosen to estimate elapsed

---

182 Andrew Snelling, *Radioactive 'dating' failure*, article from Creation magazine, Volume 22, Issue 1, 1999

183 S.A. Austin, "Excess Argon within Mineral Concentrates from the New Dactite Lava Dome at Mount St. Helens Volcano," *CEN Technical Journal*, 10(3):335-343, 1986

184 Andrew Snelling, *Radioactive 'dating' failures*, Creation magazine, Vol. 22, Issue 1, 1999

time, one can "reasonably" come up with just about any age for the Grand Canyon one wants--from 70 Ma down to 100 kyr. Given that range of error, how can modern mainstream scientists actually laugh at those who suggest a bit more recent catastrophic formation of the Grand Canyon? Who are they to scoff given such a history of huge waffles and ranges of error of their own?"[185]

Another reason to question the results of the current dating methods is the fact that new developments have come along such as the discovery that Radiohalos can form very quickly. Radiohalos are the halos of dark, colored rings in the Uranium and Polonium that is found in granite. These were believed to take 100 million years to form. It has now been discovered that they can actually form in six to ten days.[186]

Why are evolutionists so adamant on dating most things in the millions of years? It is because their theory of evolution requires millions or even billions of years to be feasible. That is the only way the theory of evolution works. With evolutionists, the idea is that given enough time, say billions of years, anything is possible.

Geologic column: The ten strata systems that geologists use compose the "standard geologic column" and are claimed by many to contain the major proof of evolutionary theory.

The standard geologic column was devised before 1860 by catastrophists who were creationists. Adam Sedgewick, Roderick Murchison, William Coneybeare, and others determined that the earth was formed largely by catastrophic processes and that the earth and life were created. They concluded that these strata layers were the same worldwide. No matter where you dug on the earth, you would encounter the same layers of strata, and they would be in the same order.

Charles Lydell and others took this much further by naming each layer based upon layer location and fossils found within that layer. Fossils played an important role in the development of the geologic column. It was assumed that by identifying the order of fossil succession, as life evolved, would determine the age

---

185 Sean D. Pitman, M.D., *The Geologic Column*, http://www.detectingdesign.com, August 2005, updated March 2010

186 Andrew Snelling, Radiohalos-*Startling evidence of catastrophic geologic processes on a young earth,* Creation magazine, volume 28, Issue 2, March 2006.

of a particular strata and its place in the geologic column. Their assumption was that the rocks containing the simple fossils must be older, and the rocks containing more complex fossils must be younger. The stratified rocks of the earth are not named and classified on the basis of the character of these rocks, but entirely by the kinds of fossils contained within them. This would fit their evolutionary theory that over time, the simple plants and animals evolved into more complex plants and animals.

"The fact is that there is no man on earth who knows enough about the rocks or the fossils to be able to prove in any fashion fit to be called scientific that any particular kind of fossil is actually and intrinsically older or younger than any other kind. In other words, there is no one who can actually prove that the Cambrian trilobite is older than the Cretaceous dinosaur or the Tertiary mammal." [187]

Index fossils are fossils that are numerous and widely distributed. These were fossils used to determine where a strata system belonged within the geological column. They are still used extensively as an indicator of the age of a given layer. It doesn't matter what kind of rock it is or on what level it is found on. The age of the rock is determined by the fossils found in it. Radioactive dating was unknown when the geological column and the assigned age of the fossil-bearing strata were being developed. Because radioactive dating gives such a wide range of ages, dates that don't fall within the predetermined age are discarded.

Although it is claimed that evolution was not a guiding principle for the construction of the geological column in the early 1800s, the formations were nonetheless pigeonholed into slots based on *fossil succession*. In other words, the original column was not necessarily developed from lithology but mainly by a succession of index fossils.[188]

Using a bit of circular reasoning, Scientist sometimes uses the adjoining layers of strata that contain fossils and their place in the geologic column to determine the age of strata that contains no fossils. The fossils age are determined by the strata's place in the geologic column. However, the age of the rock is determined by the fossils found in it. In essence, accordingly to the evolutionist the age of the rocks is

---

187 Dr. George McCready Price, *The New Geology*, Mountain View, Ca., Pacific Press, 1923
188 Oard, Michael J., *Is the geological column a global sequence?*, Journal of Creation, Volume 24, Issue 1, 2010

determined by the fossils and the age of the fossils are determined by the rocks where they are found.

"Many people believe index fossils were supplemented by radiometric dating in the 1900s, but index fossils continue to have preeminence in dating. Radiometric dates *must agree* with the geological column, or the radiometric dates are assumed wrong for various reasons. As a result of this circular reasoning, there are countless problems."[189]

The geologic column is a graphic representation of the layers of rock that make up the earth's crust. The ten strata systems that geologists use (Cambrian, Ordovician, Silurian, Devonian, Carboniferous, Permian, Triassic, Jurassic, Cretaceous, and Tertiary) compose the "standard geologic column" Each layer of strata represented a system or period of time. In essence, the geologic column is a yardstick for measuring time in the past. Evolutionists would have us believe that this also is representative of the 4.6 billion year history of the earth.

The geologic column is nothing more than a hypothetical classification based on selected rock outcrops in Europe. It is rare, if at all, where all ten strata systems exist together and in the correct order.

"One unanswerable argument for the hypothetical character of the column is that nowhere in the world does the complete column exist. The majority of the geological periods are missing in the field."[190]

"We are only kidding ourselves if we think that we have anything like a complete succession for any part of the stratigraphical column in any one place."[191]

---

189 Bates McKee, *Cascadia: the Geologic Evolution of the Pacific Northwest,* McGraw-Hill Book Company, New York, 1972
190 John Woodmorappe, *The Geologic Column: Does It Exist?,* The True. Origin Archives, http://www.trueorigin.org/geocolumn.php, October 14, 2015
191 Derek V. Alger, *The Nature of the Stratigraphical Record,* New York, John Wiley & Sons, 1981, p. 21

134 Jerry Blount

GEOLOGIC TIME SCALE

ERA	PERIOD	EPOCH	SUCCESSION OF LIFE
CENOZOIC recent life	QUATERNARY 0 - 1 Million Years Rise of Man	Recent Pleistocene	
	TERTIARY 62 Million Years Rise of Mammals	Pliocene Miocene Oligocene Eocene	
MESOZOIC middle life	CRETACEOUS 72 Million Years Modern seed bearing plants. Dinosaurs		
	JURASSIC 46 Million Years First birds		
	TRIASSIC 49 Million Years Cycads, first dinosaurs		
PALEOZOIC ancient life	PERMIAN 50 Million Years First reptiles		
	Carboniferous — PENNSYLVANIAN 30 Million Years First insects		
	MISSISSIPPIAN 35 Million Years Many crinoids		
	DEVONIAN 60 Million Years First seed plants, cartilage fish		
	SILURIAN 20 Million Years Earliest land animals		
	ORDOVICIAN 75 Million Years Early bony fish		
	CAMBRIAN 100 Million Years Invertebrate animals, Brachiopods, Trilobites		
	PRECAMBRIAN Very few fossils present (bacteria-algae-pollen?)		

Illustrations like this one from 'Answers in Genesis' are actually made by combining pieces of the geologic column from all over the world. Geologists make many assumptions when trying to explain all of the fossils, rock layers and age of each.

"Fossils are used as the only key for placing rocks in chronological order. The criterion for assigning fossils to specific places in that chronology is the assumed evolutionary progression of life; the assumed evolutionary progression is based on the fossil record so constructed. The main evidence for evolution is the assumption of evolution!"[192]

A problem that evolutionists have is that quite often; these layers are out of sequence. In every mountainous region around the world are many examples of old strata setting on top of what are supposed to be younger strata. For example, Heart Mountain Thrust in Wyoming consists of a thirty by sixty-mile area of Paleozoic strata resting horizontally on Eocene beds, which are supposed to be 250,000,000 years younger. Heart Mountain has baffled geologists for over a hundred years. You see this supposedly older strata didn't slide downhill over younger strata, it is on top of the mountain, in fact, it is the mountain. Uniformitarian geologists have come up with several interesting 'scientific' explanations to explain how this stratum slid over the 'younger' stratum, even though there is no marks or deformities as evidence of one strata sliding over another, which would be the case following a slide of this magnitude.

There are two theories that are presently in competition. I included them simply because they are so laughable. Both assume that there was prior volcanic action. One is that friction along the sliding plane released CO from the carbonates, providing a 'gas cushion' that aided further movement. The second hypothesis suggests that friction was reduced by the heating of water within the lowermost layer, causing a 'fluid overpressure.' This heating was aided by lava extruding upward in vertical cracks. Both these hypotheses, as well as all others, are unlikely and would be impossible to test.[193]

"The Heart Mountain thrust has long been structurally perplexing because there is no known structural roots or source from which it could have been derived. Furthermore, there is no known surface fault or fault zone within or adjoining from which the thrust sheet could have been derived." [194]

---

192 Henry M. Morris, *Scientific Creationism,* El Cajon, Ca., Master Books, 1985
193 Michael Oard, *The Heart Mountain Catastrophic Slide, Journal of Creation,* 20(3):3–4 December 2006
194 H.D. Hedgren, Bioscience, September,1979, p.592, cited in Creation-Evolution Encyclopedia, *The Problem With Geological Overthrusts,* www.pathlights.com/ce_encyclopedia/Encyclopedia/12fos09.htm, 2010.

"But, as with many others, this particular overthrust is an entire mountain! Heart Mountain is a high mountain, not a plain or a low valley. It is a horizontal bed of hundreds of feet of rock resting high above the Wyoming plains, overlooking them. It would require some special type of gravity to put those billions upon billions of pounds of rock up there—and do it all so carefully that it rests there, fitted perfectly together. This 30 x 60-mile triangle of very thick rock is supposed to have wandered there ("gravitated there" is how some experts describe it) in some miraculous way from somewhere else—and then climbed up on top of all the other rocks in the plains beneath it!" [195]

Quite often 'younger' rocks are found on the bottom of rocks supposedly hundreds of millions of years 'older,' and yet appear perfectly normal. When the strata layers are upside down in the supposed sequence, it is explained by evolutionists as being an "overthrust", a condition where the older strata layer was pushed up and slid over the younger strata. It seems implausible that such a large sheet of rock could be lifted and then slide above another nearly flat surface for a distance of sixty miles and yet this is a small section compared with other areas. some are claimed to have overthrusts because of the strata layers being out of sequence that are hundreds and even thousands of square miles in size. For instance, a region of the Alps has an overthrust of four hundred and fifty square miles.

"We are perfectly safe in concluding that it is solely because the fossils occur here in the reverse of the accepted order, that we have this astounding picture of an immense mountain mass having been put "upside down over an area of 450 square miles." The "older" fossils are evidently here on top, while the younger ones are underneath, and of course some explanation must be given of this flat contradiction of the life succession theory." [196]

The Lewis overthrust, in Montana, is another example of the overthrust problem. It is massive in size at 135 miles long, 35-40 miles wide and 3 miles deep. It contains six layers of strata and is supposed to have slid into place over younger strata. Such a

---

195 H.D. Hedberg, Bioscience, September, 1979, p.598, cited in Creation-Evolution Encyclopedia, *The Problem With Geological Overthrusts*
196 George McCready Price, *Illogical Geology*, Charleston, South Carolina, Nabu Press, 2014

massive mountain would have pushed a huge debris field ahead of it. However, there is no sign of this. Nor are there any signs that an immense area of nearly horizontal rock slid sideways for a great distance over shale, without ever having disturbed it! Most mountain ranges are out of sequence to the evolutionary geological column. Rather than admit the truth, evolutionists have worked out a fantastic explanation for overthrusts. Some of the explanations given sound more science fiction than scientific. For instance, the Appalachians are supposed to have been pushed up out of the ocean. The gigantically high Matterhorn Mountain is supposed to have traveled there from 30 to 60 miles away. The high Swiss peak, the Mythen is supposed to have come all the way from Africa.[197]

The use of the geological column for dating strata into different evolutionary time periods should be an embarrassment. It is not true science; rather it is science fiction! It is based on nothing more than guesswork in the early 1800's. In fact, all dating methods are based on unproven and unprovable assumptions.

---

197 Creation-Evolution Encyclopedia, *The Problem With Geological Overthrusts*, www.pathlights.com/ce_encyclopedia/Encyclopedia/12fos09.htm, 2010.

CHAPTER 19

How Old is the Earth

HOW DO WE KNOW from the Bible, that the earth is 6000 years old? The Bible gives us a chronological and genealogical Biblical history of people and events beginning from the time of creation, throughout history. It is possible, by adjusting for the differences in calendrical systems, to figure the time from creation in Genesis to the year A.D. 1. We cannot set a precise time, since most of the time the Bible only lists the time in years, and does not include the months and days. However, we can know that the time of creation was between 3900 BC and 4200 BC, making the earth a little over 6000 years old.

Many people have come up with dates for creation, such as Gerhard Hasel (4178 BC), Isaac Newton (4000 BC), and James Ussher (4004 BC).

I believe we can calculate the age of the earth using the scriptures as follows. Solomon became king in 971 B.C. (1 Kings 2:11). In the fourth year of his reign (967 B.C.), he began to build the temple which was four hundred and eighty years after the Israelites came out of Egypt (1 Kings 6:1). *(967 + 480 = 1447 B.C.)*

The Israelites were in Egypt four hundred and thirty years (Exodus 12:41). The Law was given to the Israelite people by God through Moses at Mount Sinai in the third month after they left Egypt (Exodus Chapters 19 & 20). God's Covenant with Abraham was four hundred and thirty years before the Law was given to the Israelites (Galatians 3:17). *(1447 + 430 = 1877 B.C.)*

The Covenant with Abraham was three hundred and ninety-one years after the Flood (Genesis Chapter 11 & Genesis 17:1-2). *(1877 + 391 = 2268 B.C.)*

The Flood occurred 1656 years after the week of Creation (Genesis Chapter 5 & Genesis 7:11). *(2268 + 1656 = 3924 B.C.)* The beginning of the earth when God created it was approximately 3924 B.C. Regardless of one's chronological interpretation of the scriptures. The fact is plain, that according to the Biblical record the earth is approximately 6000 years old.

The standard secular timeline is that the earth is some 4.5 billion years old. Sadly this is accepted by many Christians, even though many may deny evolution. While many may argue that it doesn't matter which you believe, in fact, it does matter. The theory of an old earth is in direct contrast to what the Bible teaches. The Bible teaches that man was created in the 'image of God.' Man being created on the sixth day, was there at the beginning of creation. *The world was created for man.* Evolution teaches that man came along billions of years later and has no divine connection to God. Evolution denies the existence of God.

It is a shame that many Christians attempt to adapt the Bible to fit the theory of evolution. Those that refer to themselves as 'progressive creationists' believe that God used million and even billions of years to create the universe and the world to its present form. They believe that millions of years separated various kinds of living creatures.

The 'day-age theory' maintains that a 'day' was a relative term and that a day of creation was much different from the 'day' as we know it. They refer to the fact that the sun was not created until the fourth day: "And God said, *"Let there be lights in the vault of the sky to separate the day from the night, and let them serve as signs to mark sacred times, and days and years, and let them be lights in the vault of the sky to give light on the earth."* (Genesis 1:14-15) They also refer to II Peter 3:8 that *"with the Lord, one day is as a thousand years, and a thousand years as one day."*

The Bible is very clear that the first thing God created was light and he called it day and it was the first day. We read in Genesis 1:5: *"God called the light "day," and the darkness he called "night." And there was evening, and there was morning—the first day."* God created 'day' on the very first day.

From the beginning of creation, a day was the same length as our present day. In six days God completed the creation process; it was complete in every way. To say that God took millions of years to complete creation is contrary to God's word.

The 'theistic evolution' belief is that God started it all and he is still watching over his creation as it evolves. This is an absurd attempt to fit the Bible to the evolution theory. A God that is just sitting back watching evolution happen is indistinguishable from no God at all.

"What a tragedy that so many Christian leaders have been bluffed and intimidated into assuming that secular interpretations of the evidence should dictate their understanding of God's Word. And right at a point in history when there are more scientific reasons than ever to confirm the utter rationality of trusting the Bible, not evolutionary conclusions.

One thing is very clear from all this. Namely, that the erroneous belief that 'science' insists that evolution and long ages are 'fact' is the most serious challenge to biblical authority, and thus to the faith in general, that Christendom has ever faced. If even Jesus' words in Scripture can't be trusted on some issues, how are we supposed to trust anything in the Bible at all?

This is in contrast to the teaching of the Lord Jesus Christ, the Creator made flesh, as well as several of the biblical authors, which makes it plain that this is wrong—people were there *from the beginning* of creation. But in the evolutionary timeline, people have only been around for one or two million years—this puts them toward the *end* of the timeline. This means that He is most definitely claiming that the world *cannot* be billions of years old." [198]

The modern scientific premise of uniformity and evolution is that the key to understanding the distance past and the unforeseeable future is by measuring the physical and natural biological processes of today, and projecting those measurements backward or forward in time. The doctrine of uniformitarianism believes that by measuring the rates of change in the natural processes of erosion, sedimentation, radioactivity, diastrophism, decay, etc., and applying these measurements to the past, will explain the origin and formation of the earth's geologic features and even the very origin and development of the earth and universe.

---

198 Carl Wieland, *Jesus on the age of the earth,* Creation Magazine, volume 34, Issue 2, April, 2012

One of science greatest errors is the refusal to believe in creation and that the creation process was complete. The natural processes of today are not a continuation of a form of creation. Their belief that all things have progressed at the same rate since the beginning of time is simply not correct. As I mentioned before there were several distinct periods of time when the natural processes would have been altered or changed completely. First, there was the week of creation. Second was the time from the week of creation until the fall of man. This was a time when everything was perfect. There was neither creation nor decay. Third was the time after the fall of man until the flood. This was a time when decay would have been taking place, but the world then was a much more vigorous and very different from today's world. And finally, there was the flood itself and the aftermath of it. The natural process during each of these times would have been substantially different. The measurements of today's natural processes simply would not apply. The present rates of change in nature can only be applied back to shortly after the flood.

The period of the flood with the many different catastrophic events would have been particularly different. There was the world being covered with water, the billions of tons of earth that was displaced, the volcanic and tectonic eruptions. Also, the upheavals and upthrusts with the forming of mountains and vast basins which greatly changed the landscape. The oceans were enlarged, and land masses were divided. It was a time of great geological changes. How could the measurements of today's processes possibly be applied to such a time?

There is considerable evidence to support the Biblical time frame for a young earth and more is being regularly compiled as research is being completed. I have included some of it here.

Meteorites: The stars themselves speak for a young earth. Meteors are constantly falling toward earth and burning up in our atmosphere. Those that don't burn up crash to earth as meteorites.

"We only find meteorites near the surface of the earth. If the earth's sediments were deposited over hundreds of millions of years, as evolutionists believe, we should find meteorites throughout all the various levels of sediment instead of only near the surface." [199]

---

199 Peter and Paul Lalonde, 301 Startling Proofs & Prophecies, Niagara Falls, Ontario, Prophecy Partners, Inc., 1997

Shrinking Sun: For the past one hundred and fifty years, astronomers have made regular measurements of the diameter of the sun. These measurements have shown that the sun is shrinking at the rate of five feet per hour. At its rate of shrinkage, as little as 50,000 years ago the sun would have been so large that our oceans would boil. 100,000 years ago the sun would have been twice its present size. But in far less time than 50,000 years, life here would have ceased to exist. Studies have shown that if the size of the sun or the earth's distance from it, were either slightly greater or smaller, life on Earth could not exist.[200]

The earth's rotation: It has been observed since the 1700's, that the earth's rotation is slowing down. Gravitational drag forces of the sun, moon and other factors cause this. If the earth were 4.6 billion years old, the moon would be much farther away from the earth, even if it started out orbiting at the earth's surface. In fact, If the earth were billions of years old, as claimed, it would already have stopped turning on its axis! [201]

The ocean's sediment: Studies have shown that close to 25 billion tons of sediment are removed from the land and deposited in the ocean every year. At that rate, it would take less than 20 million years to completely erode all the dry land on the earth to the point that no land would be exposed above sea level. If evolution is correct and the earth is 4.6 billion years old than all the dry land should have disappeared 4 billion and 580 million years ago.

You would think that there would at least be several miles of sediment on the ocean floor. In reality, we see only hundreds of feet of sediment, suggesting a much younger world than evolutionists would have us believe.[202]

The faint young sun paradox: The Sun derives energy by the thermonuclear conversion of hydrogen into helium. Over the Sun's lifetime, the thermonuclear reactions would, according to theory, gradually change the composition of the core of the Sun and alter

---

200 Vance Ferrell, Science Vs Evolution, Altamont, Tn., Evolution Facts, Inc., 2006, p. 139
201 Peter and Paul Lalonde, 301 Startling Proofs & Prophecies, Niagara Falls, Ontario, Prophecy Partners, Inc., 1997
202 Ibid

the Sun's overall physical structure. Because of this process, the Sun would gradually grow brighter with age. Thus, if the Sun is indeed 4.6 billion years old, it should have brightened by nearly 40% over this time. This means that if billions of years were true, the sun would have been much fainter in the past. However, there is no evidence that the sun was fainter at any time in the earth's history. Astronomers call this the 'faint young sun paradox,' but it is no paradox at all if the sun is only as old as the Bible says—about 6,000 years.

Evolutionists believe that life appeared on the earth about 3.8 billion years ago. But if that timescale were true, the sun would be 25% brighter today than it was back then. This implies that the earth would have been frozen at an average temperature of −3ºC. However, most paleontologists believe that, if anything, the earth was warmer in the past.[203]

Magnetic field supports a young earth: The earth's magnetic field was caused by a decaying electric current in the earth's metallic core. A strong magnetic field is crucial for life on earth. While the magnetic field is important for navigation, it is even more important in protecting the earth by forming a protective shield around the earth. This magnetic field protects us from dangerous cosmic radiation particles that are constantly bombarding us from the sun. It is also powerful evidence that the earth could not be older than about 10,000 years.

"Physics professor Dr. Thomas Barnes noted that measurements since 1835 have shown that the field is decaying at 5% per century. "Archaeological measurements show that the field was 40% stronger in AD 1000 than today." [204]

It has been calculated that the half-life of the magnetic field is about 1,400 years; this means that it loses half of its strength every 1,400 years. If the earth were as old as the evolutionists claim the magnetic field would be non-existence and life on earth would not be possible.

"The earth's magnetism is running down. This worldwide

---

203 Jonathan Sarfati, *Our Steady Sun: A Problem For Billions of Years,* Creation Magazine, Volume 26, Issue 3, June 2004
204 Merrill, R.T., and McElhinny, M.W., *The Earth's Magnetic Field,* Academic Press, London, 1983

phenomenon could not have been going on for more than a few thousand years, despite swapping direction many times. Evolutionary theories are not able to explain properly how the magnetism could sustain itself for billions of years." [205]

Solar Drag: Our sun exerts a solar drag on the small rocks and larger particles (micrometeoroids) in our solar system. This causes these particles to spiral down into the sun and be destroyed. The sun, acting like a giant vacuum cleaner, sweeps up about 100,000 tons of micrometeoroids each day. The actual process by which this occurs has been analyzed. Each particle absorbs energy from the sun and then re-radiates it in all directions. This causes a slowing down of the particle in its orbit and causes it to fall into the sun. At its present rate, our sun would have cleaned up most of the particles in less than 10,000 years, and all of it within 50,000 years. Yet there is an abundance of these small pieces of rock, and there is no known source of replenishment.[206]

Helium in the rocks: The radioactive decay of uranium and thorium contained in rocks, produces large amounts of helium. Because helium is the second lightest element, and it does not combine with other atoms, it readily leaks out and eventually escapes into the atmosphere. Helium diffuses and leaks out so rapidly that if the earth is as old as evolutionist claim, all the helium should have leaked out of the earth's rocks billions of years ago. However, the rocks still contain large amounts of helium, proving the Bible to be the most accurate source for determining the earth's age.

"While drilling deep Precambrian (pre-Flood) granitic rocks in New Mexico, geologists extracted samples of zircon crystals…….. The crystals contained not only uranium but also large amounts of helium…….. Up to 58% of the helium that the uranium could have ever generated was still present in the crystals.

The helium leakage rate has been determined in several experiments. All measurements are in agreement. Helium diffuses so rapidly that all the helium in these zircon crystals should have leaked out in less than 100,000 years. The fact that so much helium

---

205 Sarfati, Jonathan, *The earth's magnetic field: evidence that the earth is young,* Creation Magazine, Volume 20, Issue 2, March 1998
206 Vance,Ferrell, *Science vs Evolution,* Altamont, Tn., Evolution Facts, Inc., 2006, p.131

is still there means they cannot be 1.5 billion years old, as uranium-lead dating suggests. Indeed, using the measured rate of helium diffusion, these pre-Flood rocks have an average "diffusion age" of only 6,000 (± 2,000) years."[207]

Helium in the Atmosphere: There are vast amounts of helium below the earth's crust. Helium being an extremely light gas, it is constantly seeping out of the earth and into our atmosphere. Some helium escapes into space, however, this amount is much less than what is being released into the atmosphere. Scientists are able to calculate the volume of helium atoms present in the atmosphere by allowing for the difference in what is released into the atmosphere and what is escaping into space, scientists can determine the length of time required for the present volume of helium to accumulate.

The present amount of helium in the atmosphere would accumulate in about two million years. While this is much longer than the Biblical age of the earth, we do not know the original quantity of helium. God created the earth for mankind. It is likely he would have had helium present in the atmosphere from the very beginning. It is probable that the initial conditions were very similar to those of today, although minor changes in the helium concentration may have occurred since the creation of the atmosphere. It is also possible that significant changes could have occurred during and immediately following the Flood.

Evolutionists speculate that there was no helium initially because the atmosphere was yet to form. If there was no helium present in the atmosphere initially, and the present rate of flow of helium from the earth's crust had occurred for 4.5 billion years, as the long-age evolutionary model suggests, the total mass of helium in the atmosphere would be about 2,000 times the quantity actually present in our atmosphere. The present low concentration of helium would suggest that the earth's atmosphere must be quite young.[208]

Cosmic Dust: There is a constant rate of cosmic dust particles entering the earth's atmosphere from space and then settling to the earth's surface.

---

207 Snelling, Andrew, *Helium in Radioactive Rocks*, Answers Magazine, October 2012

208 Larry Vardiman, *The Age of the Earth's Atmosphere Estimated by its Helium Content, Creation Science Fellowship, Inc.*, Pittsburgh, PA, cited in Institute for Creation Research, 1986

According to NASA, there are 200 million tons of dust coming to earth every year. If the earth were 4.6 billion years old as evolutionists claim, there would be a layer of meteoritic dust nearly a half mile in thickness over the entire world. The same would be true of the moon. In fact, one of the concerns before the moon landing was that the astronauts would sink into the dust upon landing on the moon. Of course, that didn't happen, which speaks of a very young moon, earth, and universe.[209]

Moon Dust: In the 1950's, R.A. Lyttleton, a highly respected astronomer, stated:

"The lunar surface is exposed to direct sunlight, and strong ultraviolet light and X-rays (from the sun) can destroy the surface layers of exposed rock and reduce them to dust at the rate of a few ten-thousandths of an inch per year. But even this minute amount could, during the age of the moon, be sufficient to form a layer over it several miles deep."[210]

Lyttleton has been proven correct in that solar radiation does indeed turn the moon rocks into dust. If the Earth was actually 4.6 billion years old as the evolutions claim, the dust on the moon would be at least twenty miles deep.

In view of this, our men at NASA were afraid to send men to the moon. They feared that they would be buried in dust and quickly suffocate! So NASA first sent an unmanned lander to its surface, which made the surprising discovery that there was hardly any dust on the moon! In spite of that discovery, Neil Armstrong was worried about this dust problem as his March 1970 flight in Apollo 11 neared. He feared his lunar lander would sink deeply into it and he and Edwin Aldrin would perish. But because the moon is young, there is not over 2 or 3 inches of dust on its surface! That is the amount one would expect if the moon were about 6000-8000 years old.[211]

Ocean Concentrations: We have a fairly good idea of the amount of various elements and salts that are in the oceans and also how much is being added yearly by rivers, subterranean springs, rainwater, and other sources. A comparison of the two factors points to a young age for the ocean and thus for the earth. Of the fifty-one primary

---

209 G.S. Hawkins, Ed., *Meteor Orbits and Dust,* published by NASA, 1976
210 R.A. Lyttleton, quoted in R. Wysong, Creation-Evolution Controversy, p. 175.
211 Vance,Ferrell, *Science vs Evolution,* Altamont, Tn., Evolution Facts, Inc., 2006, p.134

chemical elements contained in seawater, twenty could have accumulated to their present concentrations in 1000 years or less, nine additional elements in no more than 10,000 years, and eight others in no more than 100,000 years at the most.[212] These figures are based on the theory that none of these elements existed in the ocean at the beginning, although, they may very well have, which would shorten these times even more.

The Mississippi River Delta: The Mississippi-Missouri river system is the longest river in the world and is about 4221 miles in length. The river dumps over 20 million cubic yards of mud into the Gulf of Mexico every year, at the point where the river enters the Gulf. For this amount of sediment dumping that occurs, the Mississippi Delta is not very large. Congress commissioned General Andrew A. Humphreys to make a survey of the whole area. It was completed in 1861. The English evolutionist, Charles Lyell, had earlier made a superficial examination of the river and its delta and declared the river system to be 60,000 years old since, he said, the delta was 528 feet deep. But Humphreys showed that the actual depth of the delta was only 40 feet. Below that was the blue clay of the Gulf, and below that, marine fossils. His discovery revealed that the lower Mississippi valley used to be a marine estuary. Using Lyell's formula for age computation, Humphreys arrived at the age of about 4620 years, which would be approximately the time of the Genesis Flood.[213]

Dinosaur Soft Tissue: Research done on a supposedly 65-million-year-old Tyrannosaurus Rex named Sue has confirmed the existence of blood vessels, cells with nuclei, tissue elasticity, and intact protein fragments consistent with the creationist belief that dinosaurs died off 3000 to 4000 years ago. Research on Egyptian mummies and other old age humans have established 10,000 years as an upper limit for how long such biological tissue could survive. Such soft tissue was also found on two triceratopses, and an extinct marine reptile called a mosasaur.[214]

Where Are All the people: If as evolutionist believe, man has been present on the earth for 3.8 million years, where are all the people. Even

---

212 Vance,Ferrell, *Science vs Evolution*, Altamont, Tn., Evolution Facts, Inc., 2006, p.150
213 Vance,Ferrell, *Science vs Evolution*, Altamont, Tn., Evolution Facts, Inc., 2006, p.
214 Dr David Menton, *Soft Tissue in Fossils*, Answers Magazine, October 1, 2012

with the smallest margin of population growth in 3.8 million years our current population would number well into the trillions of people. But more important, where are all the bones? In 3.8 million years we should find large numbers of human fossils.

In only one site in South Africa, there are 800 Billion vertebrate fossils buried in the Karoo Formation.[215] There are 3000 complete or near-complete dinosaur fossils and millions of incomplete fossils.[216] If there are so many animal fossils, why are there so few human fossils in comparison? If billions of people have been living and dying for 3.8 million years, where are the bones? Or, where are the tools or weapons of war? It is inconceivable that man lived on earth for billions of years and only in the last few thousands of years did man discover that plants grow from seeds and that by planting these seeds he could have more of the plants that he desired.

I realize this topic has considerable controversy connected to it, even in the Christian community. So, let me make something clear. We do not need to know anything about creation to receive eternal life from Jesus Christ. All we need to do is to believe in Jesus as our Lord and Saviour, receive him into our lives and live to serve him.

Some of us may believe in a young 6000-year-old earth; some may believe that the earth is much older. And some may not know what to believe. I will not say that it is not important what you believe, for I believe it is very important. But the most important thing is that you have a personal relationship with Jesus Christ.

Did God create a mature earth? Did God create a new earth, or did he create a mature earth? A mature earth would contain all the necessary, various minerals and elements including natural radiation that scientists claim are the result of the combination of other minerals or the breakdown over long periods of time. The rocks would show signs of age. Possibly there would even be coal and oil reserves. There would be salt reserves. The salt being deposited today in no way compares to the quality or amount that we have from a past era. We know that God created mature plant life. He did not simply create seeds and bulbs. The Bible tells us that he created the birds of the air. They were not eggs or baby birds unable to fly;

---

215 John C. Whitcomb, and Henry M. Morris, *The Genesis Flood,* Phillipsburg, N.J., Presbyterian And Reformed Publishing Co., 1989
216 Kim Gittleson, Will we ever run out of dinosaur bones? www.slate.com, 2009

they were full grown adult birds. We know that he created mature animals, as well as the fish in the seas. There is no mention in Genesis that there was anything created that was juvenile in nature. God created Adam and Eve as adults, with adult knowledge and abilities. The Bible seems to indicate that thirty is the time when a person becomes fully adult. This was the age that Jesus started preaching and it is the age when the human body is normally its strongest. The Levites were to be thirty years old to work in the temple. David and Saul were both thirty years of age when they became king. Joseph was thirty when Pharaoh put him in charge under him. If you were to meet Adam and Eve on the seventh day of creation, you would naturally assume that they were approximately thirty years old. However, you would be terribly mistaken for Adam and Eve would in reality only be one day old. I can imagine that on day seven, scientists would have claimed the rocks were millions of years old already.

Did God create a mature earth? Are scientists looking to unravel the history of a brand new earth that in reality never existed? Just as it would be impossible to go back to Adam's and Eve's baby years, it would also be impossible to go back to what scientist today would consider a new earth and new universe to be, for they never existed.

When God finished creating the heaven and earth and the universe, God looked at all that he had made and said it was very good. God had created the perfect environment for man to reside in, for he had created the earth and all that was in it for man. Therefore, God would have created a mature earth. An earth with all the necessary elements, not only for man's survival but also for his pleasure.

God created an earth that is rotating at the right speed to support life. An earth that has the correct amount of oxygen and hydrogen. The sun is the correct distance from the earth, and the gravitational pull is compatible with mankind. If any of these were to change as little as five to ten percent, life would not be possible.

God did not create a faint sun, one that was all hydrogen and no helium, as a new sun would be. This would be out of character with his perfect creation. He would have created a mature sun with the right amount of helium to ensure that the climate on earth was pleasant for mankind.

As God was creating the earth did he also create the enormous coal, oil, and salt reserves, when he created the earth, knowing there would be a time in the future when man would need them? Think of the heat, electricity and other services that are possible because of the coal deposits. Even more important is the gas and oil reserves. Oil has made possible the automobile, aircraft, and so much more. Our lives would certainly not be the same or as easy without oil. Did a gracious God foresee our use for oil? If not, then the catastrophic events of the Flood would be the only other time since creation when such huge amounts of vegetation and marine animals could have been buried to create the abundance of coal and oil that our daily lives depend on.

We have no way to know what stage of development everything on earth was in when God created it. Were the rocks already old? Were there coal, oil, and salt reserves already? We do know that God said it was very good. Therefore it was the perfect environment for man. It was the perfect place for man to reside. It definitely was not a new earth as scientists today, would consider a new earth to be. Freshly formed from space dust and gasses.

If God had wanted to create a mature earth, one that scientists today would claim was billions of years old, he certainly could have. He is the omnipotent Creator, and there is no limit to what he can do.

CHAPTER 20

Dinosaurs and Man

EVOLUTIONISTS CLAIM THAT DINOSAURS were extinct 60 million years before man walked the earth. Any proof that man lived along with dinosaurs, simply destroys the theory of evolution. This is something that evolutionist simply will not accept. Any evidence proving that man and dinosaurs lived concurrently is met with resistance and is quickly explained away, sometimes with rather bizarre explanations. However, the proof still exists that dinosaurs were here for some time after the flood.

Jose Diaz-Bolio, a Mexican archaeologist from Mexico, found an ancient Mayan relief sculpture in Veracruz, Mexico showing a bird like creature similar to the Pteranodon. In the November 1968 Science Digest, Dr. Diaz-Bolio wrote an article entitled "Serpent-bird of the Mayans." According to Dr. Diaz-Bolio, the bird is not merely the product of Mayan flights of fancy, but a realistic representation of an animal that lived during the period of the ancient Mayans-1,000 to 5,000 years ago.[217]

Missionaries have come out of the South American jungles with stories told by natives of giant birds that closely resemble pterosaurs.[218]

The evidence seems to suggest that the Archaeopteryx, or possibly a similar ancient bird lived as a contemporary of man and did not become extinct 150 million years ago, but at most, a few thousand years ago.

---

217 Ken Hudnall & Connie Wang, *Spirits of the Border: the History and Mystery of El Paso Del Norte*, Omega Press, El Paso, Tx. 2003, p.102
218 Ibid

Alvis Delk Print
In the Sir George Series
Photo: David Lines, Creation Evidence Museum

The Creation Evidence Museum of Texas has a set of Cretaceous footprints discovered by archaeologist Alvis Delk. This fossil of Glen Rose limestone consists of a dinosaur footprint (Acrocanthosaurus) on top of an eleven-inch human footprint. The human footprint matches several other fossil footprints in the area.

The fossil was sent to a professional laboratory where 800 X-rays were performed in a CT scan procedure. Laboratory technicians verified compression and distribution features clearly seen in both prints, human and dinosaur. This removes any possibility that the prints were carved or altered.[219]

In 1968 Stanley E. Taylor and his film crew were drawn to the Paluxy Riverbed near Glen Rose, Texas due to a number of published and unpublished reports of human and dinosaur tracks together, he found many residents of the area who claimed to have seen many true human tracks in the bed of the river, the best of which had since been carried away by a flood, others badly eroded. Some of these long-time residents maintained that a number of tracks of both man and dinosaur had been removed from the river

---

219 Creation Evidence Museum of Texas, *Alex Delk Cretaceous Footprints*, Glen Rose, Tx.

during the depression, and sold. These claims were given credence by the circular holes in the river bottom from which prints had been taken--in some cases with prints of approximately human appearance still leading into and away from the holes.

In an attempt to verify these claims and to find fresh evidence, they returned in 1969 and 1970 to excavate an area now known as the Taylor Site, located a few hundred yards west of Dinosaur Valley State Park. Taylor team excavated back into the riverbank in several areas. New human-like trails, as well as fresh prints in existing trails, were found. The excavations were under previously undisturbed strata, precluding the possibility that they were carvings or man-made.

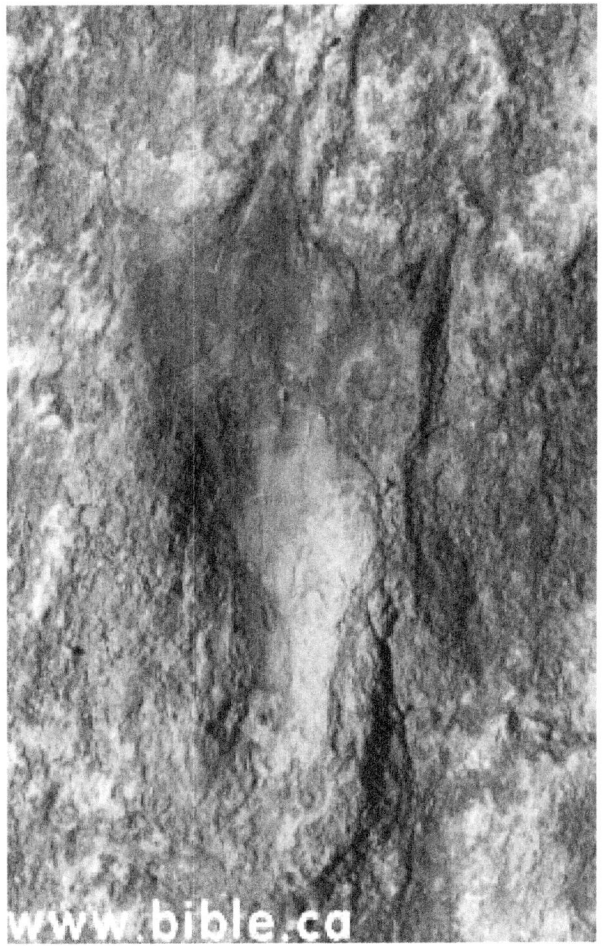

Taylor never found perfect human footprints, but did find a sequence of very human-like tracks found with at least 134 dinosaur tracks in the bed of the Paluxy River. The prints found did have significant indications of being human footprints.

This fossil footprint is one of fourteen that make up the Taylor Trail. Individual toes can be discerned in seven of the fourteen footprints.

This print is one of the most spectacular in the sequence. When examined carefully a right human footprint can be seen in compelling detail, almost completely within a dinosaur footprint[220]

---

220 www.bible.ca, *The Taylor Trail,* http://www.bible.ca/tracks/taylor-trail.htm,

There is some controversy over the Taylor site footprints. Evolutionists claim the Taylor Site tracks were elongate dinosaur tracks whose elongation was due primarily to the metatarsal impression. The fact that man and dinosaurs were contemporaries on earth is devastating to the evolutionary theory, as geologist Albert G. Ingalls stated:

"If man, or even his ape ancestors, or even that ape ancestors early mammalian ancestor, existed as far back as the Carboniferous Period in any shape, than the whole science of geology is so completely wrong that all the geologists will resign their jobs and take up truck driving." [221]

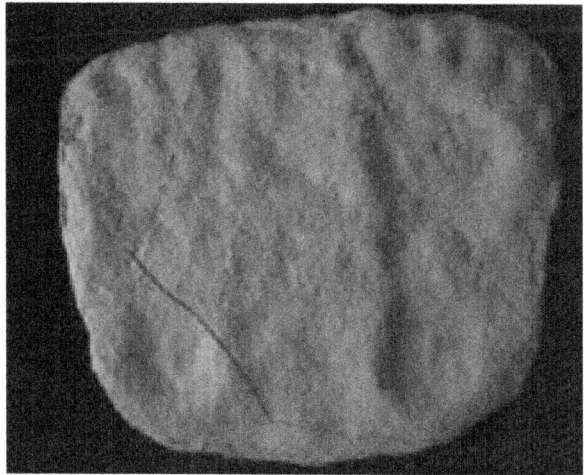

Further evidence that man lived alongside dinosaurs is a fossil human handprint shows astounding detail. Even the print of the

---

221 Albert G. Ingalls, *Scientific American,* cited in Genesis Park, *Fossil Footprints,* www.genesispark.com

thumbnail can be seen. It is also found in the same Glen Rose limestone as the footprints. This limestone is designated as Middle Cretaceous, supposedly 110 million years old and contemporary with the dinosaurs.[222]

Another fossil footprint from the Upper Carboniferous Period was reported by the head of the department at Berea College in Kentucky of a human-like track left in sandstone. Numerous scientists have investigated these tracks and concluded that they are genuine.

However, in an attempt to dismiss the tracks, the *Scientific American* article did not include the real photos in their article. Instead, they showed some pretty obvious fakes and not the actual prints, although, they had access to them. This is because, as evolutionary atheist Richard Dawkins observed, authenticated evidence of humans in the Carboniferous would "blow the theory of evolution out of the water." [223]

Skeletons of ten perfectly modern humans have been excavated from fifty-eight feet down in the Dakota Sandstone, over an area spanning about 50 by 100 feet. This formation is a member of the Lower Cretaceous, supposedly 140 million years old. It is known for its dinosaurs and is the same formation found at Dinosaur National Monument, famous for its dinosaurs.[224]

To find evidence of mammals coexisting with dinosaurs would be as devastating to the theory of evolution as humans would be, as evolutionist Richard Dawkins of Oxford stated:

"If a single, well-verified mammal skull were to turn up in 500 million-year-old rocks, our whole modern theory of evolution would be utterly destroyed." [225]

There is evidence of mammals embedded in rocks that are supposedly millions of years old, however, so far evolutionists have chosen to ignore them.

A large cat track (9 inches across) was found near Glen Rose, Texas, in the same layer with the Burdick track, Middle Cretaceous,

---

222 http://www.bible.ca/tracks/dino-fossils.htm
223 Richard Dawkins, *Free Inquiry*, vol. 21, no. 4, 2001
224 http://www.bible.ca/tracks/malachite-man.htm
225 Richard Dawkins, *The Blind Watchmaker*, W. W. Norton and company, New York, 1986, p.225

supposedly 110 million years old.[226] Fossilized horse tracks have been found in Uzbekistan along with fossilized dinosaur tracks.[227] In the Grand Canyon horse like hoofprints were visible in rocks that, according to the theory of evolution, predate hoofed animals by more than a hundred million years.[228] Hoofprints are also alongside dinosaur footprints in Virginia.[229]

In the Soviet Union scientists have reported more than 2000 fossil dinosaur footprints alongside tracks resembling human footprints. Clearly, these would have been made in the same time period in mud or similar soft earth which later hardened into rock.[230]

The fact that dinosaurs were contemporaries of man should not come as a surprise to Christians as God spoke of two creatures in the Book of Job which were obviously dinosaurs. In chapter 40, as God reprimands Job, he speaks of his own greatness and describes the Behemoth which he had created. A very large creature that had a tail like a cedar tree was not afraid of raging rivers (vs. 23), and could not be captured by man (vs. 24).

"Look at Behemoth, which I made along with you and which feeds on grass like an ox.

What strength it has in its loins, what power in the muscles of its belly! Its tail sways like a cedar; the sinews of its thighs are close-knit. Its bones are tubes of bronze, its limbs like rods of iron. It ranks first among the works of God,"(Job 40:15-19)

In chapter 41, God describes the Leviathan, a huge, fierce sea-going creature with a coat of armor and fearsome teeth. A monster that terrifies even the strong and cannot be harmed.

---

226 www.bible.ca, *Large Cat Track found at Glen Rose*, http://www.bible.ca/tracks/cat-track.htm
227 Colin Campbell-Barker, *The Square Wheel*, Xulon Press, 2005
228 Walt Brown, *In The Beginning: Compelling Evidence for Creation and the Flood*, Center for Scientific Creation, Phoenix, Az. 2001
229 Richard Monastersky, *A Walk along the Lakeshore, Dinosaur-Style*, Science News, Vol. 136, July 8, 1989, p.21
230 Alexander Romashko, *Tracking Dinosaurs*, Moscow News, No. 24, 1983, p. 10

"If you lay a hand on it, you will remember the struggle and never do it again! Any hope of subduing it is false; the mere sight of it is overpowering.............Who can penetrate its double coat of armor? Who dares open the doors of its mouth, ringed about with fearsome teeth? Its back has rows of shields tightly sealed together;............Its chest is hard as rock, hard as a lower millstone. When it rises up, the mighty are terrified; they retreat before its thrashing. The sword that reaches it has no effect, nor does the spear or the dart or the javelin. Iron it treats like straw and bronze like rotten wood. Arrows do not make it flee;............It makes the depths churn like a boiling caldron and stirs up the sea like a pot of ointment. It leaves a glistening wake behind it; one would think the deep had white hair. Nothing on earth is its equal—a creature without fear."(Job 41:8-33)

The Leviathan that God is describing may well be a plesiosaur; a large seagoing reptile that evolutionists claim was extinct millions of years before man was on earth. The Leviathan is also mentioned in Isaiah 27:1, Psalms 74:14 and Psalms 104:26.

It is evident that as God spoke to Job and his friends of the Behemoth and Leviathan, that they were aware of these creatures and that they were probably still living on earth at that time. Likewise, as David and Isaiah both spoke of the Leviathan, it must have been common knowledge that such a creature existed.

There are numerous painting and artifacts around the world of dinosaurs, many with very accurate detail. Obviously, ancient man was well aware of dinosaurs. Below are a few examples:

Bernifal Cave, one of the caverns in France that are renowned for Neanderthal artifacts, contains a picture of a dinosaur fighting a mammoth.[231]

In the San Rafael Swell, in south-central Utah, there is a pictograph that looks very much like a pterosaur. It is about 7 feet long from wingtip to wingtip, is actually painted with a dark-red pigment. Indians of the Fremont culture are thought to have inhabited the "Swell" between 700 and 1250 A.D. Black Dragon

---

231 Dr. Jack Cuozzo, *Buried Alive: The Startling Untold Story About Neanderthal Man*, Master Books, August, 2003, p. 132

Canyon is named for the pictograph which resembles a large winged reptile with a head crest.[232]

In 600 BC, under the reign of King Nebuchadnezzar, a Babylonian artist was commissioned to shape reliefs of animals on the structures associated with the Ishtar Gate. The animals appear in alternating rows with lions, fierce bulls, and curious long-necked dragons (Sirrush), which appears to be a sauropod dinosaur. These reliefs are on display in the Berlin Vorderasiatisches Museum.[233]

In 1945 archeologist Waldemar Julsrud discovered clay figurines buried at the foot of El Toro Mountain on the outskirts of Acambaro, Mexico. Eventually over 33,000 ceramic figurines were found in the area and identified with the Pre-classical Chupicuaro Culture (800 BC to 200 AD). Among the figurines were numerous figurines of dinosaurs. Moreover, the dinosaurs are modeled in very agile, active poses, fitting well with the latest scientific evidence and lending credence to the artists having actually observed these creatures. There has been considerable testing for authenticity, including extensive radiometric dating and thermoluminescent testing by the University of Pennsylvania.

There was extinct ice-age horse remains, the skeleton of a wooly mammoth, and a number of ancient human skulls found at the same location as the ceramic artifacts, validating the antiquity of the site.[234]

---

232 Dennis Swift, "Messages on Stone," Creation Ex Nihilo, vol. 19, p. 20
233 Karl Shuker, "The Sirrush of Babylon," Dragons: A Natural History, 1995, pp. 70-73
234 Charles Hapgood, *Mystery in Acambaro,* Science, February, 2000, p.82

Further evidence of the authenticity is the Iguanodon dinosaur figurine. In the 1940s and 1950s, the Iguanodon was completely unknown. It wasn't until 1978 or 1979 that skeletons of adult Iguanodons were found with nests and babies. Certainly, ancient man was aware of the Iguanodon long before modern man discovered them.

A set of cave paintings found in the Gorozomzi Hills, 25 miles from Salisbury (in Rhodesia, now Zimbabwe). For the paintings include a brontosaurus-the 67-foot, 30-ton-like creature scientists believed became extinct millions of years before man appeared on earth. However, the bushmen who did the paintings ruled Rhodesia from only 1500 B.C., until a couple of hundred years ago. And the experts agree that the bushmen always painted from life. This belief is borne out by other Gorozomzi Hills cave paintings-accurate representations of the elephant, hippo, buck, and giraffe.[235]

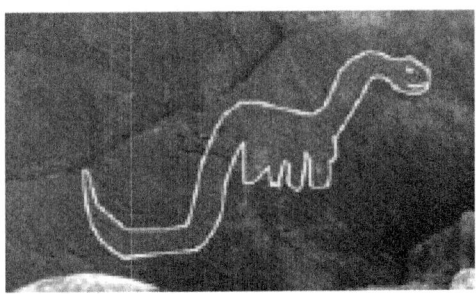

---

235 Los Angeles Herald-Examiner, *Bushmen's Paintings Baffling to Scientists,* January 7, 1970

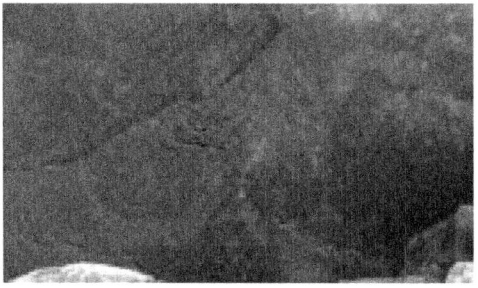

The picture above was drawn by North American Anasazi Indians that lived in the area that has now become Utah approximately 150 B.C.-1200 A.D. Even noted anti-creationists agree that it resembles a dinosaur and that the brownish film which has hardened over the picture, along with the pitting and weathering, attests to its age. One evolutionist writes, "There is a petroglyph in Natural Bridges National Monument that bears a startling resemblance to a dinosaur, specifically a Brontosaurus, with a long tail and neck, small head and all." [236]

Going even farther back in time is the fossil footprints of a human stepping on trilobites, dubbed 'The Meister Prints' near Antelope Spring, Utah.

It was the oldest fossil footprint yet found. It was discovered in June 1968 by William J. Meister on an expedition to Antelope Spring, 43 miles west of Delta, Utah. He was accompanied by his wife and two daughters and by Mr. and Mrs. Francis Shape and their two daughters. The party had already discovered several fossils of trilobites when Meister split open a two-inch-thick slab of rock

---

236 F.A. Barnes and Michaelene Pendleton, *Canyon Country Prehistoric Indians,* Wasatch Publishing,1979, p.201

with his hammer and discovered the print. The rock fell open revealing on one side the footprint of a human with at least two small trilobites (extinct, superficially crab-like arthropods) in the footprint itself. The other half of the rock slab showed an almost perfect mold of the footprint and fossils. Amazingly the human was wearing a sandal! The sandal was 10 1/4 inches long and 3 1/2 inches wide; the heel is indented slightly more than the sole, as a human shoe print would be. This was quite a surprising find since the rock at this locality is identified as the middle Cambrian Wheeler Formation--over 500 million years old.[237] This discovery has received considerable scrutiny from the evolutionists, for it is something that they simply cannot accept. To do so would destroy the theory of evolution.

Living Dinosaurs: All over the world there have been rumors and stories of living dinosaurs or dragons. The one area today that would favor living dinosaurs is the vast and unexplored swamps of equatorial Africa. Here is located the largest swamp in the world, the Likouala Swamp. Approximately 55,000 square miles, larger than the entire state of Florida, the government has officially declared it 80% unexplored. The Likouala swamp region of the Congo is supposed to be the home to the Mokele-mbembe, a water-dwelling creature that some scientists believe could be a surviving sauropod dinosaur.

Reports of dinosaur-like creatures in Central Africa go back for more than 200 years. There supposedly have been many eyewitness accounts, not only from the natives but missionaries, explorers, and scientists. The witnesses described animals that were 15 to 30 feet long, mostly head, neck and tail. The head was distinctly snake-like, a long thin tail, and the body was approximating the size of an elephant, or at least that of a hippopotamus. The legs are short, with the hind legs possessing three claws. The animals are a reddish brown in color and have a rooster-like frill running from the top of the head down the back of the neck.[238]

Though much more rare, there have been other reports coming out of the Likouala swamp region of the Congo of another dinosaur like creature, the Emela-ntouka (literally "killer of elephants"). This

---

237 Creation Evidence Museum of Texas, *The Meister Print with Trilobite*, Glen Rose, Tx.
238 William J. Gibbons. 2002. In Search Of the Congo Dinosaur. *Acts & Facts.* 31 (7)

stout rhinoceros-like creature has been known to kill elephants with its single horn. Lucien Blancou, chief game inspector in French Equatorial Africa in the 1950's wrote of a ferocious creature in the Congo, larger than a buffalo that was considered the most dangerous of animals. He stated that one was killed about twenty years earlier.[239]

And finally, new scientific evidence shows that dinosaurs were still alive just a few thousand years ago. Secular scientists have discovered about a dozen different proteins still intact inside dinosaur and other fossil bones. Some fossils even contain preserved cells, blood vessels, and skin. These surprised evolutionists because they believe these fossils are millions of years old, but these biomaterials decay far too quickly for that.[240]

There is simply too much evidence to ignore, that dinosaur, man, and the animals existed together. All were created by God during the week of creation.

---

239 Bernard Heuvelmans, On The Tracks of Unknown Animals, New York, Hill and Wang, division of Farrar, Straus and Giroux, 1959
240 Acts & Facts magazine, *Fossils: Dinosaur Proteins Project,* Volume 45, Number 3, March 2016

CHAPTER 21

The Ice Age

IN GENERAL TERMS, AN "ice age" is a time of extensive glacial activity that covers a relatively large area with ice. During the Ice Age, which ended a few thousand years ago, 30% of the land surface of the earth was covered by ice. In North America, an ice sheet covered almost all of Canada and the northern United States. We know the extent of the Ice Age because the glaciers left features on the landscape.

The flood was the greatest catastrophe in the history of the world. It involved much more than just rain and flood water. With the opening of the "fountains of the great deep" there would have been tectonic movements and seismic activity, causing tremendous volcanoes, earthquakes, and great upheavals. The surface of the earth would have been reshaped. While the flood waters, covering the entire earth only lasted a little over a year, the aftermath of the flood, earthquakes, volcanoes, upheavals, etc. would have continued for years after the waters had receded. All of the geological changes associated with the flood may not have been completed and stabilized for centuries.

A shroud of volcanic dust and particles would have been cast into the stratosphere and trapped there for several years following the Flood. These particles would have reflected some of the sunlight back to space and caused cooler summers, mainly over large landmasses. The extensive volcanic activity would have continued for many years after the Flood and gradually declined as crustal magma solidified and crustal movements lessened. There is abundant evidence of extraordinary volcanic activity during the Ice Age, which would have replenished the dust and particles in the stratosphere. Ice cores, taken from Greenland and Antarctica also show abundant volcanic particles and acids in the sections associated with the Ice Age.[241]

After the Flood, the conditions were right for the creation of the Ice Age. The waters were warm worldwide, from the moderate climate before the flood. Also, the volcanic activity and the warmer water from deep within the earth would have warmed it even more. This warm water would have resulted in great amounts of moisture being lifted up into the atmosphere. The earth's climate had changed; the earth was now much colder, with freezing temperatures over much of the earth, especially over the Polar Regions. Dust and particles from the volcanoes filled the atmosphere, blocking out the sun. All this resulted in rapid catastrophic changes to the earth's temperatures. The vast amount of moisture in the atmosphere turned to snow and began to fall upon the land for the first time since the universe was created. Conditions were right for the snow and ice to form and accumulate quickly. All these factors and others could have contributed to the rapid accumulation and growth of snow and ice over the poles and much of the northern hemisphere.

The rapidly lowering of the temperature of the polar latitudes would have frozen the water mixed with the sediments being deposited in these regions, creating those vast stretches of permanently frozen soils in the Arctic and Antarctic known as 'permafrost.'

Embedded in these frozen soils of the Arctic are large numbers of fossil mammals, trapped and in some cases frozen before the soft body parts had decayed. Some frozen mammoths still had food preserved in their mouths and stomachs

It is clear that a sharp change in climate was responsible for the freezing of so many and such a variety of mammals. An area of frozen alluvium in central Alaska contains numerous mammal fauna. The list includes bears, wolves, fox, badger, wolverine, saber-toothed cat, jaguar, lynx, wooly mammoth, mastodon, horses, camel, antelope, bison, caribou, moose, elk, sheep, musk-ox, yak, ground sloth, and rodents.[242]

---

241 Michael J. Oard, *Setting the Stage for an Ice Age*, Answers In Genesis, October 14, 2008
242 R.F, Flint, *Glacial and Pleistocene Geology*, New York, Wiley, 1957

J. K. Charlesworth stated that the New Siberian Islands have yielded mammoth, woolly rhinoceros, musk ox, saiga antelope, reindeer, tiger, arctic fox, glutton, bear and horse among the sixty-six animal species and that they would have required forest and meadows to survive. They could not have lived in a climate like the present, with its icy winds, snowy winters, frozen ground and tundra moss most of the year.[243] It is obvious that the climate was much milder before the ice age, which would fit nicely with the mild worldwide climate before the flood. It would seem that the effects of the flood triggered the conditions that resulted in the ice age immediately after the flood.

The richness of the Siberian mammoth deposits in the permafrost defies description. In Siberia alone, some 50,000 mammoth tusks have been collected and sold to the ivory trade. Ivory mines were operating for many years, and at least 20,000 tusks were taken from one mine alone. Besides mammoths, the Arctic soils contain the remains of over 60 animal species, including the woolly rhinoceros, camels, horses, tigers, and antelopes. Many of them lie in frozen silt, along with boulders and tree roots.[244]

Estimates have run as high as 5,000,000 mammoths, whose remains are buried all along the coastline of northern Siberia and into Alaska.[245]

The typical wild elephant requires over three hundred pounds of food a day. The amount of food required to feed 5,000,000 mammoths for a single day is staggering. Obviously, it would require a land very rich in plant life, which in turn would require a warm climate. Despite the popular misconception mammoths were not cold weather animals but were more suited to a mild temperate climate, the same as elephants. The Berezovka Mammoth discovered in 1901 near Siberia's Berezovka River, contained twenty-four pounds of undigested vegetation in its mouth and stomach. This vegetation consisted of grasses, shrubs, tree leaves, herbs, and mosses. Only a small percentage of the food found in Berezovka's mouth and stomach grows near the Arctic Circle today. Furthermore, the flower fragments in its stomach show that it died

---

243 J.K. Charlesworth, quoted by John C. Whitcomb and Henry M. Morris, *The Genesis Flood*, Phillipsburg,
244 Ibid
245 Henry Howorth, archaeologist, *The mammoth and the Flood*, London, Sampson Low, Marston Searle & Risington, 1887

during warm weather. Clearly, the first world was one of a subtropical climate with lush foliage and abundant food for all.[246]

"Though the ground is frozen for 1,900 feet down from the surface at Prudhoe Bay, everywhere the oil companies drilled around this area they discovered an ancient tropical forest. It was in a frozen state, not in petrified state. It is between 1,100 and 1,700 feet down. There are palm trees, pine trees, and tropical foliage in great profusion. In fact, they found them lapped all over each other; just as though they had fallen in that position." [247]

It has occasionally been suggested that the ocean waters would have remained warm for too long a period to allow for the preservation of the soft parts of the animals, the inference being that they must have perished in some other catastrophe centuries later. However, it is doubtful that post-flood Siberian climates could ever have supported such vast hordes of animals.

"The animals that perished in the flood did not, of course, have to float around on the Arctic Ocean for months, but were quickly buried in the depositional silts of the flood waters. The entrapped waters in these sediments, cut off from the warm waters of the open ocean, froze rapidly, forming the "permafrost",the permanently frozen soils and subsoils of the Arctic lands, and it was in these that the mammals and other animals of the region was buried. As Charlesworth says: "The frozen mammals are found on the timbered banks of rivers and in soil that nearly always contains fragments of trees. Bacterial decay was hindered by the cold climate and by quick interment in fine silts."[248]

On the other hand, most of the animals did suffer decay and thus may have been exposed for some time prior to burial.

There is most certainly no modern parallel entombment of elephants or any other kind of mammal taking place anywhere in the modern world. It may not be quite clear as yet whether these deposits were made directly during the Deluge period or soon after, or both, but it seems fairly evident that the extermination of such immense hordes of animals and their internment in what has ever since been frozen soil must be somehow explained in terms of the

---

246 John Keyser, *Earth Rings and Frozen Mammoths,* Hope of Israel Ministries, Temple City, Ca. 2012
247 Lindsey Williams, *The Energy Non-Crisis,* 2nd. Edition, 1980, p. 54
248 John C. Whitcomb and Henry M. Morris, *The Genesis Flood,* Phillipsburg, N.J., Presbyterian And Reformed Publishing Co., 1989

events accompanying just such a universal aqueous catastrophe as the Bible describes.[249]

While the catastrophic nature of the flood being the mechanism to induce glaciation and the ice age is unacceptable to many geologists, it does fit within that framework and seems more probable than anything offered by uniformitarianism.
Based on what we know about the impact of the global Flood on the continents, sediments, and climate, it is clear that an ice age would not require hundreds of thousands to millions of years, as stipulated by evolutionary beliefs. Moreover, it is unnecessary to accept the current complicated evolutionary ideas of about thirty separate ice ages over the past 2.5 million years.[250]

---

249 Ibid
250 Michael Oard, *Setting the Stage for an Ice Age,* Answers Magazine, Volume 2 No. 2 April-June 2007

CHAPTER 22

Noah's sacrifice and God's covenant

CAN YOU IMAGINE HOW Noah and his family felt when they embarked from the Ark realizing that they were the only people on earth? The world they had known was gone. Gone were the people, the cities, the animals, and the civilization they had known. What a lonely feeling it must have been. On the one hand there must've been sadness realizing the loss of lives, but on the other hand, there had to be great joy that God had saved them.

The first act of Noah was to build an altar, and offer a sacrifice of thanksgiving unto God for saving and protecting them. Noah used some of the clean animals and clean birds and offered burnt offering unto God. God was pleased with Noah's offering. The scriptures say the Lord *"smelled the pleasing aroma"*. God was pleased with Noah and made a covenant with him. The covenant was with Noah and his descendants. In essence it was with all mankind from the time of Noah to today. God said that never again would he curse the earth because of man.

> God said to Noah and his sons; *"I now establish my covenant with you and with your descendants after you and with every living creature that was with you—the birds, the livestock and all the wild animals, all those that came out of the ark with you—every living creature on earth. I establish my covenant with you: Never again will all life be destroyed by the waters of a flood; never again will there be a flood to destroy the earth."* (Genesis 9:9-11)

God said that he would give mankind a sign *"This is the sign of the covenant ………I have set my rainbow in the clouds, and it will be the sign of the covenant between me and the earth. Whenever I bring clouds over the earth and the rainbow appears in the clouds, I will remember my covenant between me and you and all living creatures of every kind. Never again will the waters become a flood to destroy all life. Whenever the rainbow appears in the clouds, I will see it and remember the everlasting covenant between God and all living creatures of every kind on the earth."* (Genesis 9:12-17)

God said that when he sees the rainbow, he would remember his covenant with man. It was for man's benefit that he said this, for it would be impossible for God to forget.

If any part of the human race survived the flood other than Noah and his family, they would not have been included in the covenant God made with Noah. Genesis tells that God's covenant was with Noah, his descendants, and all the birds and animals that were on the Ark with him.

The implication is (vs. 10), *"every living creature on earth,"* that the only creatures on the earth were those from the Ark. In verse twelve, God again implies that the only creatures or people on earth were those on the Ark and that all mankind from this time forward would be descendants of Noah.

Noah's sacrifice was pleasing to God, as his life had been. In return, God made a covenant with Noah, his family and for all generations to come. That includes you and me, our families and descendants. When we see a rainbow, we can know that it represents a promise that God not only made to Noah, but to you and I as well.

CHAPTER 23

Where is the Ark?

GENESIS 8:4 SAYS THAT after the flood waters subsided, "the ark came to rest on the mountains of Ararat." While the Biblical text says "mountains" (plural), therefore referencing a range rather than an individual mountain, many have tried to identify the specific mountain on which Noah's ark came to rest. Mount Ararat, the highest peak of the Armenian Highlands, is a dormant volcano located in eastern Turkey near the border with Iran and Armenia.

Titus Flavius Josephus, a first-century historian, although not a believer, has recorded many events of the Bible which took place during his lifetime. In his book, *Antiquities of the Jews,* Josephus wrote about the ark:

> "the ark rested on the top of a certain mountain in Armenia ... However, the Armenians call this place, αποβατηριον 'The Place of Descent'; for the ark being saved in that place, its remains are shown there by the inhabitants to this day. Now all the writers of barbarian histories make mention of this flood, and of this ark; among whom is Berossus. For when he is describing the circumstances of the flood, he goes on thus: "It is said there is still some part of this ship in Armenia, at the mountain of the Cordyaeans; and that some people carry off pieces of the bitumen, which they take away, and use chiefly as amulets for the averting of mischiefs." Hieronymus the Egyptian also, who wrote the Phoenician Antiquities, and Mnaseas, and a great many more, make mention of the same."[251]

---

251 Titus Flavius Josephus, *The Testimonium Flavianum, Antiquities of The Jews,* 1.3.5-6, Translated by. William Whiston, A.M. Auburn and Buffalo. John E. Beardsley, 1895

In 280 BC, Berossus, a Chaldean priest wrote Babyloniaca, (The History of Babylonia). In it, he clearly states that the location of Noah's ark was common knowledge and that people climbed Mount Ararat to collect pieces of wood to be used as lucky charms to ward off evil. We have no extant manuscripts of Berossus books. However, much of his writing exists through citations by others writers who have quoted from his books. Those that have quoted from him concerning the ark are Abydenus (200 BC), Apollodorus (160 BC), Alexander Polyhistor (50 BC), Josephus (110 AD), Georgius Syncellus (800 AD), Eusebius, (325 AD). It shows that Noah's ark is a historical fact since many people had seen it with their own eyes.[252]

There have been many accounts of seeing the Ark down through the years. Obviously for there to be so many stories of ark sightings, there must be something there. The following accounts are just a few of these stories.

Russian aviator: In 1942, much interest was created when Russian aviators made a detailed report of the discovery of the Ark. This was in the early part of World War II, and the world's attention was focused on the war.

While parts of this story may be fictional, later investigations have confirmed the primary details.[253]

This discovery was said to be made by Mr. Vladimar Roskivitsky, a converted Russian aviator, who escaped from the Bolsheviks and came to America. The following is an account as told by Mr. Roskivitsky and reprinted in the *Banner* of the Reformed Church, dated November 27, 1942.

"It was in the days just before the Russian revolution that this story really begins. A group of us Russian aviators were stationed at a lonely temporary outpost about twenty-five miles northwest of Mount Ararat. The day was dry and terribly hot, as August days so often are in this semi-desert land.

"Even the lizards were flattened out under the shady side of rocks and twigs, their mouths open and tongues lashing out as if each panting breath would be their last. only occasionally would a tiny wisp of air rattle the parched vegetation and stir up a choking

---

252 Steve Rudd, *The Search for Noah's Ark*, www.noah's-ark.tv, 2014
253 Violet M. Cumming, *Has Anybody Really Seen Noah's Ark?*, San Diego, Creation-Life Publishers, 1982, pp. 61-108

cloudlet of dust.

"Far up on the side of the mountain, we could see a thundershower, while still farther up we could see the white snow cap of Mount Ararat, which has snow all year around because of it's great height. How we longed for some of that snow!

"Then the miracle happened. The captain walked in and announced that plane number seven had it's new supercharger installed and was ready for high altitude tests and ordered my buddy and me to make the tests. At last, we could escape the heat!

"Needless to say, we wasted no time getting on our parachutes, strapping on our oxygen cans, and doing all the other half dozen things that have to be done before 'going up.'

"Then a climb into the cockpits, safety belts fastened, a machinist gives the prop a flip and yells 'contact,' and in less time than it takes to tell it we are in the air. No use wasting warming up the engine when the sun already has it nearly red hot.

"We circled the field several times until we hit the fourteen-thousand-foot mark and then stopped climbing for a few minutes while to get used to the altitude.

"I looked over to the right at the beautiful snow-capped peak, now just a little above us, and, for some reason I can't explain, turned and headed the plane straight for it.

"My buddy turned around and looked at me with question marks in his eyes, but there was too much noise for him to ask questions. After all, twenty-five miles doesn't mean much at one hundred miles an hour.

"As I looked down at the great stone battlements surrounding the lower part of the mountain, I remembered having heard that it had never been climbed since the year seven hundred before Christ, since some pilgrims were supposed to have gone up to scrape tar off an old shipwreck to make good luck emblems to wear around their necks to prevent their crops from being destroyed by excessive rainfall. The legend said they had left in haste after a bolt of lightning had struck near them and had never returned. Silly ancients! Who ever heard of looking for a shipwreck on a mountaintop?

"A couple of circles around the snow-capped dome, and then a long swift glide down the south side, and then we suddenly came upon a perfect little gem of a lake, blue as an emerald, but still frozen over on the shady side. We circled around and returned for another look at it. Suddenly my companion whirled around and yelled something and excitedly pointed down at the overflow end of the lake. I looked and nearly fainted.

A submarine? No, it wasn't, for it had stubby masts, but the top was rounded over with only a cat walk about five feet across down the length of it.

"What a strange craft, built as if the designer had expected the waves to roll over the top most of the time and had engineered it to wallow in the sea like a log, with those stubby masts carrying only enough sail to keep it facing into the waves! (Years later, in the Great Lakes, I saw the famous 'Whaleback' ore carriers with the same kind of rounded deck.)

"We flew down as close as safety permitted and took several circles around it. We were surprised when we got close to it at the immense size of the thing, for it was as long as a city block and would compare very favorably with the modern battleships of today. It was grounded on the shore of the lake with about one-fourth of the rear end still running out into the water, and its extreme rear was three-fourth under water. It had been partly dismantled on one side near the front, and on the other side there was a great door nearly twenty feet square, but with the door gone. This seems quite out of proportion as even today's ships seldom have doors even half that large.

"After seeing all we could see from the air, we broke all speed records back to the airport.

"When we related our find, the laughter was loud and long. Some accused us of getting drunk on too much oxygen, and there were many other remarks too numerous to relate.

"The captain, however, was serious. He asked several questions and ended by saying, 'take me up there, I want to look at it.'

"We made the trip without incident and returned to the airport.

"What do you make of it? I asked as we climbed out of the plane.

"Astounding,' he replied, 'do you know what ship that is?'

"Of course not, sir."

"Ever hear of Noah's Ark?'

"Yes sir, but I don't understand what the legend of Noah's Ark has to do with us finding this strange thing fourteen thousand feet up on a mountaintop.'

"This strange craft,' explained the captain 'is Noah's Ark. It has been sitting up there for nearly five thousand years. Being frozen for nine or ten months of the year, it couldn't rot and has been on cold storage, as it were, all this time. You have made the most amazing discovery of the age."

"When the captain sent his report to the Russian government, it aroused considerable interest, and the Czar sent two companies of soldiers to climb the mountain. One group of fifty men attacked on one side, and the other group of one hundred men attacked the mountain from the other side.

"Two weeks of hard work was required to chop out a trail along the cliffs of the lower part of the mountain, and it was nearly a month before the Ark was reached.

"Complete measurements were taken and plans drawn of it as well as many photographs, all of which were sent to the Czar of Russia.

"The Ark was found to contain hundreds of small rooms and some large with high ceilings. The large rooms usually had a fence of great timbers across them, some of which were two feet thick, as though designed to hold beasts ten times as large as elephants, somewhat one sees today at a poultry show; only instead of chicken wire, they had rows of thinly wrought iron bars across the front.

"Everything was heavily painted with a wax like paint resembling shellac, and the workmanship of the craft showed all the signs of a high type of civilization.

"The wood used throughout was oleander, which belongs to the cypress family and never rots, which of course, coupled with the facts of it being painted, and it being frozen most of the time, accounted for it's perfect preservation.

"The expedition found on the peak of the mountain above the ship, the burned remains of timbers which were missing out of one side of the ship. It seemed that these timbers had been hauled up to the top of the peak and used to build a tiny one-room shrine, inside of which was a rough stone hearth like the altars the Hebrews used for sacrifices, and it either caught fire from the altar or been struck by lightning, as the timbers were considerably burned and charred over and the roof was completely burned off.

"A few days after this expedition sent its report to the Czar, the government was overthrown and the godless Bolshevism took over, so the records were never made public and probably destroyed in the zeal of the Bolsheviks to discredit all religion and belief in the truth of the Bible.

"We Russian of the air fleet escaped through Armenia, and four of us came to America where we could be free to live accordingly to the 'good old book,' which we had seen for ourselves to be absolutely true, even to as fantastic sounding a thing as a world flood.[254] This is the story exactly as published and allegedly told by Mr. Roskivitsky. In February 2000, Joseph Kulik, an alleged expedition member, was interviewed. Details he provided duplicate those of other accounts.[255]

Porcher Taylor: Porcher Taylor, an associate professor in paralegal studies at the University of Richmond's School of Continuing Studies in Virginia. He has been searching for the Ark through satellite imagery since 1973, forty-one years ago, when he was a junior cadet at West Point. He came across "credible rumors" ricocheting off the walls of the academy that a CIA spy satellite had accidentally imaged "what appeared to be the bow of a ship sticking up out of the ice cap on Mt. Ararat." [256]

The CIA refers to this object as the 'Ararat Anomaly.' It was first photographed by fixed-wing aircraft in 1949, by a U-2 in 1956, and by satellites in 1973, 1976, 1990, and 1992. Thanks to Taylor's efforts, some of the early photographs have been released to the public.

Whatever it is, the anomaly of interest rests at 15,300 feet (4,663 meters) on the northwest corner of Mt. Ararat, and is nearly submerged in glacial ice. It would be easy to call it merely a strange rock formation.

The Genesis blueprint of the Ark detailed the structure as 6:1 length to width ratio (300 cubits by 50 cubits). The anomaly, as viewed by satellite, is close to that 6:1 proportion.

English Scientists: In 1856 three English scientists climbed Mount Ararat to prove that the Ark did not exist. They got a young Armenian boy, Haji Yearman, and his father to guide them to the ark, which they did. This upset the scientists because their object was to prove that the ark was not there. They tried to burn and destroy it, but they were unable do so. Then they threatened Haji Yearman and his father with persecution if they ever told of this expedition.

---

254 Alfred M. Rehwinkel, *The Flood: In the Light of the Bible, Geology, and Archaeology*, St. Louis, Mo., Concordia Publishing House, 1951
255 Walt Brown, *In The Beginning: Compelling Evidence for Creation and the Flood*, Center for Scientific Creation, Phoenix, Az. 2001
256 Leonard David, *Noah's Search: Probing Satellite Imagery for Lost Ark*, Space.com, http://www.space.com/26318-noah-ark-search-satellite-images.html, 2014

Later one of the English scientists while on his deathbed stated that as a young man in 1856 he and two other scientists climbed the mountain of Ararat and saw the Ark of Noah. Meanwhile, Haji Yearman had moved to California and converted to Christianity. Near the end of his life, he told of him and his father guiding the English scientists and of their finding the Ark.

The two separate accounts coincided perfectly, authenticating the expedition and the finding of the ark.[257]

Turkish Explorers: Newspaper clippings from the New York Times, Chicago Tribune, and several other papers around the world tell the story of a group of Turkish explorers who climbed the mountain in 1883 and stumbled onto the ark of Noah. After receiving the explorer's report, the Turkish government sent an expedition consisting of several Turks and one English commissioner.

Upon climbing the mountain, they found the ark and entered it through a hole in the side wall. After de-icing the first three compartments, they reported that inside there were cages large enough to keep animals.[258]

George Greene: In 1953, Greene, an oil geologist, took several photographs of the Ark from a helicopter. After returning to the United States, Greene was unable to raise financial backing for a ground-based expedition. Shortly after that, he lost his life in British Guiana. All of his possessions were missing.[259]

Gregor Schwinghammer: Gregor Schwinghammer claims he saw the Ark from an F-100 aircraft in the late 1950s, while assigned to the 428th Tactical Fighter Squadron based in Adana, Turkey. Schwinghammer said it looked like an enormous boxcar lying in a gully high up on Mount Ararat.[260]

Ron Wyatt: One of the more notable reported discoveries of the Ark was by amateur archaeologist Ron Wyatt in 1987.

It began in 1959 when Turkish army captain Llhan Durupinar discovered an unusual shape while examining aerial photographs of

---

257 Kelly L Segraves, *The Search for Noah's Ark*, Beta Books, 1975
258 Ibid
259 Ibid
260 Ibid

his country. In September 1960, twenty-seven-year-old Ron Wyatt read an article in Life Magazine concerning the discovery of this strange boat-shaped formation in the mountains of Ararat. It was not Mount Ararat, but twelve miles away on another peak in the mountains of Ararat. The object is actually on Cudi Dagi mountain which is translated "Doomsday Mountain."

Below is an insert from that article:

"While routinely examining aerial photos of his country, a Turkish army captain suddenly gaped at the picture shown above. There, on a mountain 20 miles south of Mt. Ararat, the biblical landfall of Noah's Ark, was a boat-shaped form about 500 feet long. The captain passed on the word. Soon an expedition including American scientists set out for the site.

At 7,000 feet, in the midst of crevasses and landslide debris, the explorers found a clear, grassy area shaped like a ship and rimmed with steep, packed-earth sides. Its dimensions are close to those given in Genesis: 'The length of the ark shall be 300 cubits, the breadth of it 50 cubits, and the height of it 30 cubits,' that is, 450x75x45 feet. A quick two-day survey revealed no sign that the object was man-made. Yet a scientist in the group says nothing in nature could create such a symmetrical shape. A thorough excavation may be made another year to solve the mystery." [261]

---

261 Wyatt Museum, wyattmuseum.com, *Noah's Ark?*, 2011

In 1977 Ron Wyatt visited the site. After obtaining official permission, Ron and others conducted more thorough research over a period of several years. In 1978, an earthquake in Eastern Turkey exposed more of the object.

Evenly spaced indentations could be seen around the object, which looked like decaying rib timbers. Of course, everything had petrified and turned to stone. They used metal detection surveys, subsurface radar scans, and chemical analysis. Some of their findings were startling. Metal detectors revealed the presence of a regular pattern of metal readings both along the top and sides for the entire length of the ship. Its length is exactly 515 feet in the length, the same as the Arks 300 cubits if using the royal cubit, which is the measurement Noah was likely to have used. Radar scans showed internal structures which were completely consistent with the inside of a ship containing rooms and chambers, as well as three decks. (Photo below reveals the lighter color rib timbers in a systematic, vertical pattern.)

A hole drilled into the side of the object. Core samples revealed cat hair, an unknown fiber thought to be plant fiber, and an obvious man-made fiber. Included in these core samples were petrified animal dung, a petrified antler and a piece of a beam that actually appears to be three pieces of plank laminated together. Examination reveals the glue oozed from the layers. The outside of the wood appears to have been coated with bitumen. Laboratory analyses revealed that the petrified wood contained iron nails embedded in the wood. It would appear that knowledge of construction was far beyond anything we knew existed in the ancient world. The Iron Age is usually placed at 1200-1000 BC, yet we have iron nails being used in this extremely old construction. We know that before the flood man had knowledge of metalworking, the Bible makes mention of this when it speaks of Tubal-Cain, a descendant of Cain, who forged all kinds of tools of bronze and iron.[262] Wyatt's team also discovered large disc shaped rivets. From simple observation of the metal, it was possible to see where the rivet had been hammered after being inserted through a hole. (photo below)

---

262 Ibid

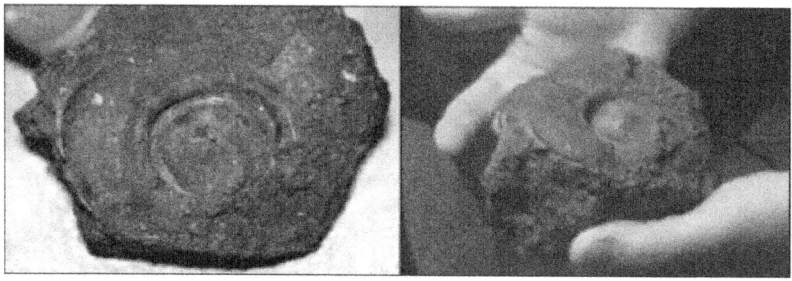

The rivets revealed that they were a combination of iron, aluminum, and titanium. Aluminum does not exist in the metallic form in nature. This implies an extremely advanced knowledge of metallurgy.

Also discovered in the area are many large anchor stones. These stones, weighing many tons, have holes carved in them.

Scientists have determined that they were anchors and the holes would have been their attachment to a ship with hemp rope. These were hung off the rear of the vessel to keep it in line with the waves

Even though the scientific community has for the most part ignored these findings, the evidence seems to indicate that this could very well be the Ark of Noah.

The Turkish government has verified Mr. Wyatt's tests, and has given him credit for the discovery. They officially declared it a national park. The announcement appeared in Turkey's largest newspaper on June 21, 1987. It has since been upgraded from a national park to the status of a national treasure. The government has built a visitors center overlooking the site and have official tourist brochures.[263]

There is considerable more information on the internet pertaining to this site. I urge you to research it further. From all the evidence so far, this could indeed be the Ark. It would be nice if the scientific community got involved and done more in depth testing. Of course, that will never happen. In the third chapter of 2nd. Peter, the Bible tells us that in the latter days, they will scoff at the idea of the flood and the Ark.

Chinese and Turkish explorers: The latest reported discovery of the Ark as reported on FoxNews.com, is by a group of Chinese and Turkish evangelical explorers. They claim the wooden remains they have discovered on Mount Ararat in eastern Turkey are the remains of Noah's Ark.

On April 25, 2010, a press conference was held in Hong Kong to announce to the world's media that the Ark had been discovered at 13,000 feet on Mt. Ararat. At the press conference, wood, rope and white pellet samples were on display. The five-page press release was entitled: "Exploration team successfully ventures inside a 4,800-year-old wooden structure on snow-capped Mt. Ararat. Experts and Turkish officials believe the artifact is Noah's Ark." The group claims that carbon dating proves the relics are 4,800 years old, meaning they date to around the same time the ark was built.

Yeung Wing-Cheung, from the Noah's Ark Ministries International research team that made the discovery, said: "It's not 100 percent that it is Noah's Ark, but we think it is 99.9 percent that this is it."

According to the research team, the structure contained several compartments; some with wooden beams that they believe were used to house animals. They ruled out an established human settlement on the grounds none have ever been found above 11,000 feet in the vicinity.

During the press conference, team member Panda Lee describes visiting the site, "In October 2008, I climbed the mountain with the Turkish team. At the elevation of more than 4,000 meters, I saw a

---

263 Ark Discovery International, Inc., Sparta, Tn., http://www.arkdiscovery.com/noah's_ark.htm

structure built with plank-like timber. Each plank was about eight inches wide. I could see tenons, proof of ancient construction predating the use of metal nails. We walked about one hundred meters to another site. I could see broken wood fragments embedded in a glacier, and some twenty meters long. I surveyed the landscape and found that the wooden structure was permanently covered by ice and volcanic rocks."

Dutch Ark researcher Gerrit Aalten stated: "There's a tremendous amount of solid evidence that the structure found on Mount Ararat in Eastern Turkey is the legendary Ark of Noah."

A Full-length feature films has been produced by the discovery team, publicizing their claim to have found the Ark on Mt. Ararat, proclaiming that the biblical record is, therefore, true, and are sharing the Gospel on that basis. The film is also being used to raise funds for further exploration and documentary production, with the same evangelistic purposes. The premiere screening was in Sydney, Australia, with the film being subsequently shown in other Australian capital cities, including recently in Brisbane. Other film showings have occurred in Hong Kong and Taiwan, and now the film is being released in the USA.

Local Turkish officials are appealing to the central government in Arakara for protection of the site while an archaeological dig is conducted.[264]

We will have to wait on this latest claim to the discovery of the Ark, to see what the archaeology dig produces. From the pictures I have seen so far, it is hard to tell what you are looking at as most everything is encased in ice.

Not everyone in the Christian community believes this find to be the ark. Dr. Andrew Snelling had this to say:

"If the wooden remains of the Ark were to be found on Mt. Ararat, then samples of that wood would be expected to yield C-14 dates of between 20,000 years and 50,000 years, consistent with the C-14 dates of pre-Flood wood found fossilized in the geologic record of the Flood. Even though the true age of such fossilized pre-Flood wood should be only 4,500, it must be concluded that these wood samples cannot have come from the pre-Flood wood used to build the Ark. Given the present C-14 evidence, despite the tantalizing wooden remains the

---

264 FoxNews.com, *Has Noah's Ark Been Found on Turkish Mountaintop?* http://www.foxnews.com/scitech/2010/04/27/noahs-ark-found-turkey-ararat/, April 27, 2010

Chinese-Turkish team claims to have discovered on Mt. Ararat, such artifacts CANNOT have come from the Ark. So whatever they have found, they are NOT the remains of the Ark." [265]

Throughout history, there have been many accounts of people having seen the Ark. As Christians, we would love absolute proof that the Ark has been discovered to prove to the world that the story of Noah and the Ark is true. However, we need to understand that the world will never accept the Ark as fact no matter how much evidence they are exposed to. The world is full of proof of God, His Son Jesus and His glorious creation, but the world will not accept this proof. They reject the idea that there is a God who will one day judge the world. They deny there was a worldwide flood and that Noah and his family were saved on the Ark. They deny the judgment by water and the coming judgment by fire. This will not change until the Lord returns (2 Peter 3:3-10).

---

265 Dr. Andrew A. Snelling, *Is the Wood Recently Found on Mt. Ararat from the Ark?*, Answers in Genesis, November 9, 2011

CHAPTER 24

God's Final Judgement

WHILE THE FLOOD WAS God's judgment upon the antediluvian earth, it was also a cleansing from the evil and sin that existed then. While it was a watery grave for the inhabitants of the earth that turned their back on God, and sought their own evil desires, it was deliverance for those on the Ark from the sin and corruption that was engulfing their lives.

Just as the flood was God's judgment upon a sinful world, the final judgement of fire will likewise, be God's judgment upon man's continual desire to sin against him. Just like before the flood, we live in a fallen, wicked world. A world where people have turned his back on God. A world where men are yielding to their greed, lust, pride, and selfish sinful nature.

> Jesus said: *"As it was in the days of Noah, so it will be at the coming of the Son of Man. For in the days before the flood, people were eating and drinking, marrying and giving in marriage, up to the day Noah entered the ark; and they knew nothing about what would happen until the flood came and took them all away. That is how it will be at the coming of the Son of Man."* (Matthew 24:37-39)

The point Jesus is making here is that man will be so busy fulfilling his own desire and pleasures, that there will be no time for God. He will live his life as if there is no God. He will laugh at those who follow the Lord. We see this all around us today. Christians are being labeled as fanatics, ignorant, extremist and more. Peter warned us of this:

> "Above all, you must understand that in the last days scoffers will come, scoffing and following their own evil desires." (2 Peter 3:3)

Peter warned that man would forget about the judgment by the flood. Man has not only forgotten that it happened, but he is denies that it ever happened.

> "But they deliberately forget that long ago by God's word the heavens came into being and the earth was formed out of water and by water. By these waters also the world of that time was deluged and destroyed. By the same word the present heavens and earth are reserved for fire, being kept for the day of judgment and destruction of the ungodly." (2 Peter 3:5-7)

Jesus said that people would be so self-involved and self-centered that just like before the flood, he will be unaware of the coming doom and judgment until it is too late. Our God is a God of love and grace to those that love and obey him. But he is a just God who cannot abide sin and wickedness. If he did not spare the angels when they sinned and he did not spare the perfect world he had created for man, how then, can the wicked and ungodly expect to escape his wrath on the final day of judgment?

The good news is that we don't have to face this judgment. We don't have to face the all-consuming fire. Christ has made it possible for us to be with him in paradise.

In my book, *Things You Probably Didn't Learn In Church*, I included a section on the end time events and the events leading up to it. Bible scholars agree, we are very near to the end times. I would not be surprised to witness this in my lifetime. All prophecy leading up to the start of the end times has been fulfilled. The next prophecy to be fulfilled will be the rapture. The rapture will be when Christ returns to take the believers home to heaven. This will mark the beginning of the tribulation. The only reason God has not returned yet is because he doesn't want anyone to be lost (2 Peter 3:9). We are truly living in a period of grace.

Make sure you are ready when Jesus returns.

Christ has made it easy for us by dying for us. He paid for our sins with his blood.

> *"But God demonstrates his own love for us in this: While we were still sinners, Christ died for us. Since we have now been justified by his blood."* (Romans 5:8-9)

First, admit you are a sinner, we all are (Romans 3:23). And then ask Christ to forgive you of your sins, believing that Jesus Christ is the Son of God, and you will be saved.

> *"That if you confess with your mouth, "Jesus is Lord," and believe in your heart that God raised him from the dead, you will be saved."* (Romans 10:9)

If you have done this, you are now a child of God.

> *"Yet to all who received him, to those who believed in his name, he gave the right to become children of God."* (John 1:12)

Live to please God, enjoy your abundant life in him, and I will see you in heaven.

PHOTOS & ILLUSTRATIONS

Page 42	Image from Egypt Origins
Page 74	Photo from geological survey of Canada
Page 76	Photo courtesy of Center for Scientific Creation
Page 98	Photo from www.gettyimages.com
Page 117	Photo of Amazing Bible Discoveries, www.6000years.org
Page 119	Photo courtesy of NationalGeographic.com
Page 134	Illustration by Answers in Genesis
Page 154	Photo from Creation Evidence Museum
Page 155	Photo courtesy of www.bible.ca
Page 156	Photo courtesy of www.bible.ca
Page 157	Photo credit belongs to creationist researcher Ian Juby
Page 157	Photo courtesy of www.bible.ca
Page 161	Images compliment of 6000years.org
Page 161	Images compliment of 6000years.org
Page 162	Top photos by historysevidenceofdinosaursandmen.weebly.com
Page 162	Bottom photo provided by Clifford Burdick, 1982
Page 163	Photo courtesy of Wyatt Museum, wyattmuseum.com
Page 163	Photo courtesy of Wyatt Museum, wyattmuseum.com
Page 182	Photos courtesy of www.viewzone.com
Page 183	Top photos compliments of Wyatt Museum, wyattmuseum.com
Page 185	Bottom photo courtesy of Ark Discovery.com

BIBLIOGRAPHY

Abbott, WJ Lewis, *The ossiferous fissures in the valley of the Shode, near Ightham, Kent,* Quarterly Journal of the Geological Society 50.1-4 (1894): 171-187.
Acts & Facts magazine, *Fossils: Dinosaur Proteins Project,* Volume 45, Number 3, March 2016
Alger, Derek V., *The Nature of the Stratigraphical Record,* New York, John Wiley & Sons, 1981, p. 21
All About Science, Big Bang Theory-An Overview, http://www.allaboutscience.org/big-bang-theory.htm, 2015
Amazing Bible Discoveries, *www.6000years.org,* 2015
American Museum of Natural History, cited in Rehwinkel, Alfred M.,*The Flood,* St. Louis, Mo., Concordia Publishing House, 1951
Ancient Mesopotamians.com, *Ancient Mesopotamian Ships, Boats for River Transportation,* 2013
Answers in Genesis, *Safety Investigation of Noah's Ark in a Seaway,* Journal of Creation 8, no. 1, April, 1994.
Answers in Genesis, News to Note, April 21, 2007, A Tree for Today?
Answers in Genesis, November 9, 2011
Austin, Allen, *Antediluvian civilizations,* www.genesis.allenauston.net/antediluvian.htm., 2006
Austin, S.A.,*Excess Argon within Mineral Concentrates from the New Dactite Lava Dome at Mount St. Helens Volcano, CEN Technical Journal,* **10**(3):335-343, 1986)
Austin, Steven A., *Ten Misconceptions About the Geologic Column,* Acts & Facts 13 (11), 1984
Austin, Steve A., *Mount St. Helens and Catastrophism,* Acts & Facts 15 (7), 1986

Arnold, C.A., *An Introduction to Paleobotany*, cited in Henry M. Morris, *Studies in the Bible and Science*, PA., Presbyterian and Reformed Publishing Co., 1966.
Ark Discovery International, Inc., Sparta, Tn., http://www.arkdiscovery.com/noah's_ark.htm,
Ashton, John, *Evolution Impossible*, Master Books, Green Forest, Ar., 2012
Barnes, F.A., and Pendleton, Michaelene, *Canyon Country Prehistoric Indians*, Wasatch Publishing,1979, p.201
BBC News, *Fisherman catches 'Living Fossil'*, August 1, 2007, http://news.bbc.co.uk
BBC NEWS Science-Nature 9/25/2003 http://news.bbc.co.uk
Beardsley, Tim, *Fossil Bird Shakes Evolutionary Hypotheses*, Nature, Vol. 322, 21 August 1986
Blount, Jerry, *Things You Probably Didn't Learn In Church*, Bloomington, IN., WestBow Press, 2015
Briney, Amanda, Geography.About.com, *The Great Salt Lake and Ancient Lake Bonneville*, 2015
Brown, Walt, *In The Beginning: Compelling Evidence for Creation and the Flood*, Center for Scientific Creation, Phoenix, Az. 2001
Campbell-Barker, Colin, *The Square Wheel*, Xulon Press, 2005
Charles Lydell, *The Geological Evidence of The Antiquity of Man*, Charleston, South Carolina, BiblioBazaar, 2009
Charlesworth, J.K., quoted by John C. Whitcomb and Henry M. Morris, *The Genesis Flood*, Phillipsburg,
Collett, Sidney, *All About The Bible*, Westwood, N.J., Barbour And Company, 1989.
Cox, Ben B., "Transformation of Organic Material Into Petroleum Under Geological Conditions," Bulletin of the American Association of Petroleum Geologists, May 1946, p. 647
Creation Evidence Museum of Texas, *Alex Delk Cretaceous Footprints*, Glen Rose, Tx.
Creation Evidence Museum of Texas, *The Meister Print with Trilobite*, Glen Rose, Tx.
Creation-Evolution Encyclopedia, *The Problem With Geological Overthrusts*, www.pathlights.com/ce_encyclopedia/Encyclopedia/12fos09.htm, 2010.
Cumming, Violet M., *Has Anybody Really Seen Noah's Ark?*, San Diego, Creation-Life Publishers, 1982, pp. 61-108

Cuozzo, Jack, *Buried Alive: The Startling Untold Story About Neanderthal Man*, Master Books, August, 2003, p. 132

Darwin, Charles, *The Origin of Species*, Skyros Publishing, ,2015, p. 80 & 157

David, Leonard, *Noah's Search: Probing Satellite Imagery for Lost Ark*, Space.com, http://www.space.com/26318-noah-ark-search-satellite-images.html, 2014

David, Leonard, Exclusive: *Satellite Sleuth Closes in on Noah's Ark Mystery*, Space.com, http://www.space.com/2134-exclusive-satellite-sleuth-closes-noah-ark-mystery.html, 2006 ,

Dawkins, Richard, *Free Inquiry*, vol. 21, no. 4, 2001

Dawkins, Richard, *The Blind Watchmaker*, W. W. Norton and company, New York, 1986, p.225

Denton, Michael, *Evolution: A Theory in Crisis*, London, Burnett Books, 1985, p 330-331

Dickerson, R.E., *J. Molecular Evolution*, 34:277, 1992, Perspective on Science and the Christian Faith, 44:137-138,1992

Dunbar, C.O., *Historical Geology, Second Edition*, John Wiley, New York, 1960, p. 47.

Evolution Facts Inc., Evolution Encyclopedia Volume 2, *Effects of the flood*, Part 1 Chapter 19

Evolution Facts Inc., Evolution Encyclopedia Volume 2, *Effects of the flood*, Part 2 Chapter 19

Feduccia, Alan. *The origin and evolution of birds*. Yale University Press, 1999.

Feduccia, Alan, cited by Joe White and Nicholas Comninellis, *Darwin's Demise*, Green Forest, Ar., Master Books, 2001

Ferrell, Vance, *Science vs Evolution*, Altamont, Tn., Evolution Facts, Inc., 2006.

Finkel, Irving, *The Ark Before Noah: Decoding The Story of the Flood*, New York, Nan A. Talese/Doubleday, 2014

Flint, R. F., *Glacial and Pleistocene Geology*, New York, Wiley, 1957

Fodor, Jerry, *Why Pigs Don't Have Wings*, London Review of books, vol. 29, no. 20, 2007, p.19-22

Fodor, Jerry, and Piattelli-Palmarini, Massimo, *What Darwin Got Wrong*, New York, Farrar, Straus, and Giroux, 2010

FoxNews.com, *Has Noah's Ark Been Found on Turkish Mountaintop?*, http://www.foxnews.com/scitech/2010/04/27/noahs-ark-found-turkey-ararat/, April 27, 2010

Fricke, Hans, "Coelacanths: The Fish That Time Forgot," *National Geographic*, Vol. 173, June 1988, p. 837.

Gallup Poll, *Americans' views related to religiousness, age, education*, http://www.gallup.com/poll/170822/believe-creationist-view-human-origins.aspx, 2014

Genesis Park, *Ancient Human Skeletons*, http://www.genesispark.com, 2015

Gibbons. William J., 2002. In Search Of the Congo Dinosaur. *Acts & Facts*. 31 (7)

Gillispie, Charles C., *Genesis and Geology*, Cambridge, Harvard University Press, 1951.

Gittleson, Kim, *Will We Ever Run Out of Dinosaur Bones?*, www.slate.com, 2009

Glueck, Nelson, *Rivers In The Desert: History of Negev*, New York, Farrer, Straus, and Cadahy, 1959.

Gould, Stephen Jay, *The Ediacaran Experiment*, Natural History No. 93, February 1984, p.14-23.

Gould, Stephen Jay, *Ever Since Darwin*, W.W. Norton, New York, 1977, p161-162

Gould, Stephen Jay., *The Panda's Thumb*, W. W. Norton & Company (1992), pp. 181-2.

Haaretz, *Sa'ar Dismisses Chief Scientist For Questioning Evolution*, Oct. 5, 2010, www.haaretz.com

Ham, Ken, *Did Adam Have a Belly Button*, Green Forest, Ar, Master Books, 2009

Hapgood, Charles, *Mystery in Acambaro*, Science, February, 2000, p.82

Hautier, Lionel, and Cox, Philip G., Rodentia: a model order?, Evolution of the Rodents, Cambridge University Press, 2015, p.4

Hawkins, G.S., Ed., *Meteor Orbits and Dust*, published by NASA, 1976

Hedberg, H. D., cited in Creation-Evolution Encyclopedia, *The Problem With Geological Overthrusts*, www.pathlights.com/ce_encyclopedia/Encyclopedia/12fos09.htm, 2010.

Hedberg, H.D.,Bioscience, September, 1979, p.598, cited in Creation-Evolution Encyclopedia, *The Problem With Geological Overthrusts*

Heuvelmans, Bernard, On The Tracks of Unknown Animals, New York, Hill and Wang, division of Farrar, Straus and Giroux, 1959

Howorth, Henry Hoyle, *The Mammoth and the Flood*, Whitefish, Montana, Kessinger Publishing, 2010

Howorth, Henry, *The mammoth and the Flood*, London, Sampson Low, Marston Searle & Risington, 1887

Hoyle, Fred and N. Chandra Wickramasinghe, *Archaeopteryx, the Primordial Bird: A Case of Fossil Forgery*, Swansea, England, Christopher Davies, Ltd., 1986

Hudnall, Ken & Wang, Connie, *Spirits of the Border: the History and Mystery of El Paso Del Norte*, Omega Press, El Paso, Tx. 2003, p.102

Huxley, Julian, *Essays of a Humanist*, Harper & Row, New York, 1964, pp.82-83

Ingalls, Albert G., *Scientific American,* cited in Genesis Park, *Fossil Footprints*, www.genesispark.com

Josephus, Flavius, *The Testimonium Flavianum, Antiquities of The Jews*, 1.3.5-6, Translated by. William Whiston, A.M. Auburn and Buffalo. John E. Beardsley, 1895

Kerr, R.A.,*Pathfinder Tells a Geologic Tale with One Starring Role,* Science, 09 Jan 1998: Vol. 279, Issue 5348,

Keith, M.L. and Anderson, G.M., *Radiocarbon Dating: Fictitious Results with Mollusk Shells,* Science, August 16, 1963, p.634

Keyser, John, *Earth Rings and Frozen Mammoths*, Hope of Israel Ministries, Temple City, Ca. 2012

Kinnaman, J.O., *Diggers For Facts*, Haverhill, MA., Destiny Publishers, 1945.

Kinns, Samuel, *Moses and Geology: Or, the Harmony of the Bible with Science*, Ulan Press, 2012

Kitts, David B., *Search for the Holy Transformation,* quoted from Institute for Creation Research, *Scientific Creationism*

Labonde, Peter and Paul, *301 Startling Proofs & Prophecies*, Niagara Falls, Ontario, Prophecy Partners, Inc., 1997

Lewontin, Richard, Review of the Demon-Haunted World, by Carl Sagan. In New York Review of Books, January 9, 1997.

Lieb, E.H. and Yngvason, Jakob, "A Fresh Look at Entropy and the Second Law of Thermodynamics," Physics Today (vol. 53, April 2000), p. 32.

LiveScience.com, *Found! Hidden Ocean Locked Deep In Earth's Mantle*, www.livescience.com, *2014*

Los Angeles Herald-Examiner, *Bushmen's Paintings Baffling to Scientists,* January 7, 1970

Lyttleton, R.A., quoted in R. Wysong, Creation-Evolution Controversy, p. 175.

Maryland Department of Natural Resources, http://dnr.maryland.gov/naturalresource/fall2006/cave.

Marshall, Logan, *Our National Calamity of Fire, Flood and Tornado*, L.T.Meyers, 1913, Amazon Indie Digital Publishing

McKee, Bates, *Cascadia: the Geologic Evolution of the Pacific Northwest*. McGraw-Hill Book Company, New York, 1972

Menton, David, *Can Evolution Produce an Eye? Not a Chance!*, Missouri Assoc. for Creation, Inc., 1994

Menton, David, *Soft Tissue in Fossils*, Answers Magazine, October 1, 2012

Merrill, R.T., and McElhinny, M.W., *The Earth's Magnetic Field*, Academic Press, London, 1983

Miller, William J., *An Introduction to Historical Geology*, New York, Van Nostrand, 1952

Millot, Jacque, *The Coelacanth, Scientific American*, Vol. 193, Dec. 1955, p. 37

Mitchell, Elizabeth, *Tropical Huntsman, Answers in Genesis*, May, 2011

Monastersky, Richard, *A Walk along the Lakeshore, Dinosaur-Style*, Science News, Vol. 136, July 8, 1989, p.21

Moreland, J.P., *The Creation Hypothesis: Scientific Evidence for an intelligent designer*, Downers Grove, Il, InterVarsity Press, 2016, p.98-99

Morris, Henry M., Scientific Creation, Master Books, El Cajon, Ca. 1985

Morris, Henry M., *Studies In The Bible And Science*, Philadelphia, PA., Presbyterian and Reformed Publishing Co., 1966.

Morris, Henry M. and Martin E. Clark, *The Bible Has The Answers*, Green Forest, AR., Master Books, 2005

Morris, Henry M.,*The Biblical Basis for Modern Science*, Green Forest, AR., Master Books, 2002

Morris, Henry M. *The Scientific Case Against Evolution*, Institute For Creation Research, http://www.icr.org/home/resources/resources_tracts_scientificcaseagainstevolution/

Morten, O., *Flatlands*, New Scientist, 159(2143), July, 1998

Mortenson, Terry, *The Key to the Age of the Earth*, Answers Magazine, Oct. 13, 2008, pp. 62–65 Myers, Norman, *The End of the Lines*, Natural History, Vol. 94, Feb. 1985, p 2

National Geographic, *Deep Sea Hydrothermal Vents,* www.education.nationalgeographic.com, 2014

National Oceanic and Atmospheric Administration, *How much water is in the ocean,* http://oceanservice.noaa.gov/facts/oceanwater.html, 2014

N.W. Creation Network, *Flood Legends from Around the World,* www.nwcreation.net, 2014.

Oard, Michael J., *Is the geological column a global sequence?,* Journal of Creation, Volume 24, Issue 1, 2010

Oard, Michael J., *Setting the Stage for an Ice Age,* Answers In Genesis, October 14, 2008

Oard, Michael, *Setting the Stage for an Ice Age,* Answers Magazine, Volume 2 No. 2 April-June 2007

Oard, Michael, *The Heart Mountain Catastrophic Slide,* Journal of Creation, 20(3):3-4 December 2006

O.D. von Engeln and K.E. Caster, *Geology,* New York, McGraw-Hill,1952,pp. 256-257.

Pappas, Stephannie, *5 Battles in the War Between Creationism and Evolution,* www.livescience.com, February 4, 2014

Patterson, Colin, as cited in Jonathan Sarfati, *Refuting Evolution,* Green Forest, Ar. Master Books, 1999

Pittman, Sean D., M.D., *The Geologic Column,* http://www.detectingdesign.com, August 2005, updated March 2010

Price, Dr. George McCready, *Illogical Geology,* Charleston, South Carolina, Nabu Press, 2014

Price, Dr. George McCready, *The New Geology,* Mountain View, Ca., Pacific Press, 1923

Provine, Will, "No Free Will," in Catching Up with the Vision, ed. by Margaret W. Rossiter, Chicago: University of Chicago Press, 1999, p. S123. U.S.Geological Survey, *The Water Cycle: Water Storage in the Atmosphere,* http://water.usgs.gov/edu, 2014

Raup,David M., *Conflicts between Darwin and Paleontology, Field Museum of Natural History Bulletin,* Jan. 1979

Raup, David M., *Evolution and the Fossil Record, Science,* Vol 213, July 17,1981

Rehwinkel, Alfred M., *The Flood: In the Light of the Bible, Geology, and Archaeology,* St. Louis, Mo., Concordia Publishing House, 1951

Roach, John, National Geographic News, April 18, 2007

Romashko, Alexander, *Tracking Dinosaurs*, Moscow News, No. 24, 1983, p. 10 Boyce Rensberger, *How the World Works*, NY, William Morrow, 1986, p18

Rudd, Steve, *The Search for Noah's Ark*, www.noah's-ark.tv, 2014

Ruse, Scott M., *The Collapse of Evolution*, Grand Rapids, Mi., Baker Books, 2011

Ryan, William & Pittman, Walter, *Noah's Flood*, New York, Simon & Schuster, 1999

Sagan, Carl, *The Dragons of Eden*, New York, Random House, 1977

Salet, G, *Hasard et Certitude: Le Transformisme dent la Biologie Actuelle*, 1973, p. 331.

Sarfati, Jonathan D., *Refuting Evolution*, Green Forest, Ar.,Master Books, 2002, p53

Sarfati, Jonathan, *The earth's magnetic field: evidence that the earth is young*, Creation Magazine, Volume 20, Issue 2, March 1998

Sarfati, Jonathan, *Our Steady Sun: A Problem For Billions of Years*, Creation Magazine, Volume 26, Issue 3, June 2004

Schwabe, Christian, On the Validity of Molecular Evolution, *Trends in Biochemical Sciences*, July 1986, p. 282

Science, *Dehydration melting at the top of the lower mantle*, Vol 344, Issue 6189, 13 June 2014, Pp.1265-1268

Segraves, Kelly L., *The Search for Noah's Ark*, Beta Books, 1975

Shuker, Karl P.N., "The Sirrush of Babylon," Dragons: A Natural History, 1995, pp. 70-73

Swift, Dennis, "Messages on Stone," Creation Ex Nihilo, vol. 19, p. 20

Todd, Scott C., *A View from Kansas on the Evolution Debates*, Nature, Vol. 401, September 30, 1999, p. 423.

Shea, James H.,"Twelve Fallacies of Uniformitarianism," in Geology, September 1982, p. 457.

Sherwin, Frank, *Biology and the Age of the Earth*, Institute for Creation Research, 2004

Simpson, George Gaylord, *The Major Features of Evolution*, New York, Columbia University Press, 1953

Simpson, George Gaylord, *Tempo and Mode in Evolution*, New York, Columbia University Press,1944, p.106

Singham, Mark, "Teaching and Propaganda," Physics Today, Vol. 53, June 2000, p. 54.

Snelling, Andrew A., *Can Flood geology explain thick chalk beds?*, article from Journal of Creation, volume B, issue 1, April 1994.

Snelling, Andrew A.,*Carbon-14 in Fossils, Coal and Diamonds,* Answers Magazine, October 2012

Snelling, Dr. Andrew, *Is the Wood Recently Found on Mt. Ararat from the Ark?,* Answers in Genesis, November 9, 2011

Snelling, Andrew, *Helium in Radioactive Rocks,* Answers Magazine, October 2012

Snelling, Andrew, *Radioactive 'dating' failure,* Creation magazine, Volume 22, Issue 1, 1999

Snelling, Andrew, *Radiohalos-Startling evidence of catastrophic geologic processes on a young earth,* Creation magazine, volume 28, Issue 2, March 2006.

Snelling Andrew, A.,*10 Best Evidences From Science That Confirm a Young Earth,* Answers Magazine, October-December 2012

Suess, Eduard, *Face of the Earth,* cited by, Price, George McCready, *Illogical Geology,* Rochester, N.Y., Scholar's Choice, 2015

Stanley, Steven M., *The New Evolutionary Timetable,* New York, Basic Books Inc., 1981, p.95

Stoner, Peter W., *Science Speaks,* Chicago, Moody Press, 1969.

Swinton, W.E., *Biology and Comparative Physiology of birds,* A.J. Marshall, Ed., New York, Academic Press, 1960, Vol. 1, p.1, quoted from Henry Morris, *Scientific Creationism*

Thomas, Lowell, *Hungry Waters, The Story of The Great Flood,* Philadelphia, The John C. Winston Co., 1937

Toussaint, Marcel, *The painful agony of the Evolutionist Myth: Scientific Weaknesses of the Evolution Theory,* BookRix, Amazon Digital Services LLC, 2016

Twain, Mark, *Life on the Mississippi,* Amazon Digital Services LLC, 2012

Vail, Isaac Newton, *The waters above the firmament,* Publisher Cleveland, O., Clark & Zangerle, 1902, digitized by Google from the library of the New York Public Library

Vardiman, Larry, *The Age of the Earth's Atmosphere Estimated by its Helium Content,* Creation Science Fellowship, Inc., Pittsburgh, PA, cited in Institute for Creation Research, 1986

Velikovsky, I., *Earth in Upheaval,* New York, Doubleday and Co., 1955.

Wallace, Alfred Russell, *The Geographical Distribution of Animals,* London, Macmillan and Company, 1876

Whitcomb, John C., *The Early Earth,* BMH Books, winona Lake, In., 2011.

Whitcomb, John C. and Morris, Henry M., *The Genesis Flood*, Phillipsburg, N.J., Presbyterian And Reformed Publishing Co., 1989
White, E.G., *Noah-Another Storm Is Coming*, Coldwater, MI., Remnant Publications, 2014
Wieland, Carl, *Jesus on the age of the earth*, Creation Magazine, volume 34, Issue 2, April, 2012
Wikipedia, *Fossil Butte National Monument*, http://en.wikipedia.org/wiki/Fossil_Butte_National_Monument, 2011
Wikipedia, *Lake Agassiz*, http://en.wikipedia.org/wiki/Lake_Agassiz, 2015
Wikipedia, *Submarine Canyons*, http://en.wikipedia.org/wiki/Submarine_canyon, 2015
Wikipedia, *World Population*, http://en.wikipedia.org/wiki/World_population, 2015
Williams, Lindsey, *The Energy Non-Crisis*, 2nd. Edition, 1980, p. 54
Wilson, Clifford, Ebla: Its Impact on Bible Records, Acts and Facts, 6 (4), 1977
Wilson, E.O., *The Humanist*, September/ October, 1982, p40
Wood Bryant G., *Great discoveries in Biblical Archaeology: The Sumerian King List, B Spade 16:4, Fall 2003, p. 120*
Woodmorappe, John, *The Geologic Column: Does It Exist?*, The True. Origin Archives, http://www.trueorigin.org/geocolumn.php, October 14, 2015
Woodruff, David S., *Evolution: The Paleobiological View*, Science, Vol. 208, 16 May 1980, p. 716.
Woolley, Leonard, *Ur of The Chaldees*, InExile Publishing, 2012
www.bible.ca, *Malachite Man*, http://www.bible.ca/tracks/malachite-man.htm
www.bible.ca, *Fossilized Hand Print*, http://www.bible.ca/tracks/dino-fossils.htm
www.bible.ca, *The Taylor Trail*, http://www.bible.ca/tracks/taylor-trail.htm,
www.bible.ca, *Large Cat Track found at Glen Rose*, http://www.bible.ca/tracks/cat-track.htm
Wyatt Museum, wyattmuseum.com, *Noah's Ark?*, 2011

Printed in Great Britain
by Amazon